THE GARLIC COOKBOOK

David DiResta

BRISTOL PUBLISHING ENTERPRISES
San Leandro, California

A Nitty Gritty® Cookbook

Printed in the United States of America.

ISBN 1-55867-108-0

Cover design: Frank Paredes
Cover photography: John Benson
Food stylist: Suzanne Carreiro
Illustrator: James Balkovek

CONTENTS

Acknowledgments

To Joanne Foran for sharing her cheerfulness, tireless work ethic, creativity, innovative cooking techniques and generosity.
To all garlic growers, purveyors and cooks throughout the world.
To all my friends and family who are always there for me.

INTRODUCTION

Never has there been a vegetable as varied in flavors and mysterious in folklore as the intriguing garlic bulb. Cultivated since ancient times for its cooking versatility and medicinal qualities, the garlic bulb continues to capture the imaginations of creative cooks and diners just about everywhere. Since 1979, when the first garlic festival was held in Gilroy, California, also known as the garlic capital of the world, annual celebrations have cropped up in New York, Virginia, Arizona and Washington. Often referred to as "the scented pearl" or "the stinking rose," each year more and more garlic is being consumed, and the trend is increasing. Farmers throughout the world are growing a vast number of garlic bulbs to fill the demand for this fascinating member of the lily family, which includes onions, shallots, leeks and chives.

Since garlic is harmonious with most herbs and spices, it complements meats, poultry, seafood and vegetables beautifully. Whether baked, sautéed, roasted, fried or raw, garlic is an ingredient used in many cuisines, including Italian, Chinese, French, Greek and Middle Eastern.

GARLIC VARIETIES

With a reputation for an intense and penetrating aroma, today's garlic crop is actually quite extensive, making it possible to have fresh garlic year-round.

The white bulb (*Allium sativum*), called American or California garlic, produces very intense cloves.

The purple and rose bulbs (*Allium sativum*), called Mexican or Italian garlic, also produce strong cloves.

The large, white elephant bulb (*Allium ampeloprasum*) yields milder cloves than other varieties. An elephant garlic bulb can grow up to the size of an orange, with cloves weighing 1 ounce each.

Rocambole is a wild cousin of garlic, with over 450 species. Its cloves have a mild flavor. Rocambole grows in serpentine forms, primarily in Europe and Asia. It is called by many names, including top-setting, serpent, giant or French garlic. Rocambole is rarely commercially available in the United States.

Green garlic is young garlic before it begins to form cloves. It has a milder flavor, so more is usually needed. The tops can be thinly sliced and used as an excellent garnish for salads and cooked foods.

COOKING GARLIC

Various cooking methods alter the flavor of garlic substantially. Slowly baking a bulb of garlic will lessen the garlic pungency to a soft and mellow, sweet-tasting flavor. Raw garlic, which can be overly powerful, should be added sparingly in very small pieces to cold salads, soups, pastas and hot crusty breads. Minced garlic or garlic squeezed through a press, added to the ingredients prior to baking or sautéing, will add a distinctive savory flavor and aroma to the dish. Garlic burns easily, however, and overly sautéed or burnt garlic will be bitter and should be discarded.

PURCHASING GARLIC

When purchasing garlic, be sure it's fresh and firm. I prefer to purchase nonpackaged individual bulbs, thus avoiding the soft, spongy bulbs that have rotted and lost flavor. If stored properly, garlic should remain fresh for up to one month. Keep garlic in a cool, dry place but not in the refrigerator. A well-vented ceramic pot creates the ideal environment to ensure freshness. Don't separate the cloves from the bulb or peel the garlic until you are ready to use it in the recipe. If a garlic bulb should start to sprout it's still fine to consume. However, the flavor will not be as intense, so the quantity may have to be increased.

Fresh garlic is far superior to dehydrated and processed forms, but there are occasions when fresh garlic is not available or does not mix well with other ingredients.

In most dishes, dehydrated minced and chopped garlic, or garlic flakes, should be reconstituted with liquid before using; however, they can be added "as is" to liquid-based dishes, such as sauces and soups.

Dehydrated garlic, when ground to a powder, combines well with flour, breadcrumbs or spices and adds a nice flavor when lightly sautéed with foods. One-eighth teaspoon dehydrated powder, minced or chopped garlic, or garlic flakes, is equal to 1 fresh clove.

Garlic salt is about 90 percent salt and should be used in place of salt in a recipe. About ½ teaspoon garlic salt will substitute for 1 fresh clove.

To ensure freshness, purchase all forms of dehydrated garlic in tightly sealed jars and store them in a cool, dark area with your other spices. Garlic powder and garlic salt have a limited shelf life of approximately 2 to 3 months. When they are too old, they impart an "off" flavor.

Garlic extract and garlic juice come from garlic cloves squeezed through a press and separated from the crushed garlic. These are intense and mix well with other ingredients.

Preminced or prechopped garlic preserved in liquid and sold at supermarkets in small jars is fairly close to fresh garlic and is convenient when you don't have much time to prepare a meal.

Although these are all acceptable means of adding a garlic taste to cooked and raw foods, unfortunately there is no substitute for the wonderful and unique flavor of garlic prepared from fresh, firm cloves.

HEALTH BENEFITS

It's absolutely fascinating that something so delicious could possible be so good for you. Garlic's written history on medicinal uses is the largest and one of the oldest of any cultivated plant. It has a reputation as a purifying herb, used as an internal as well as an external bactericide (bacteria killer) and vermifuge (parasitic worm killer).

Among the many recent facts about health benefits associated with garlic is the astounding data from the medical study at the New York Medical College of Valhalla, New York, which released research that proves that eating as little as ½ to 1 clove of garlic a day will cut blood cholesterol by 9 percent. It was shown that garlic reduces LDL-cholesterol (the "bad" kind) and increases HDL-cholesterol (the "good" kind).

It is still not clear, however, how garlic bestows health benefits, and there is still a question of whether some of garlic's beneficial elements are destroyed by heat or processing.

GARLIC FACTS AND FOLKLORE

- In Hunan province in China, some people eat more than 50 pounds of alliums a year, including garlic, onions, scallions and chives.[1]
- The Egyptian Pharaohs gave garlic to the slave laborers who built the pyramids because it was said to prolong physical strength.
- Primarily due to its odor, garlic has historically been associated with the lower classes, and although up until the 20th century it has been taboo for the elite to consume garlic, the peasantry viewed it as an all-purpose preventive medicine.
- In Sweden, superstitious farmers tied garlic around cow's necks to keep trolls from stealing the milk.

1. Susan Belsinger and Carolyn Dille. *The Garlic Book* (Loveland, CO: Interweave Press, 1993), 12.

- In some religions, including sects of Christianity, Islam and Zen Buddhism, garlic's odor as it leaves the body is associated with the devil, evil spirits and uncleanliness.[2]
- In Egyptian times, 15 pounds of garlic bought a healthy male slave.[3]
- Garlic was used as an antiseptic to treat wounded soldiers during World War I.
- Garlic braids have offered a convenient and decorative method of storing garlic bulbs (and in some cultures, keeping evil spirits at bay) for centuries. Braid garlic by the stalks, removing bulbs one at a time, as needed.
- Garlic's pungent odor comes from diallyl disulfide, a sulfur compound that is activated by contact with oxygen. It is easily absorbed by the body and permeates the lung tissue.
- Raw garlic lingers in the body longer than cooked garlic.
- Antidotes for garlic breath include breath mints, parsley, fennel and chlorophyll tablets. These have limited effectiveness since garlic's odor is also released through the pores.
- Be careful to use proper canning methods when canning garlic. Improper canning can release the bacterium that causes botulism and can cause fatal food poisoning.

2. Belsinger and Dille. *The Garlic Book*, 11.
3. Michael Castleman. *The Healing Herbs* (Emmaus, PA: Rodale Press, 1991), 177.

- Cut garlic by hand with a high-carbon stainless steel knife (see page 14). This releases only a small amount of the oil. Food processors can unevenly smash the cloves, which gives up too much of the oil and causes a harsher flavor.

- If you do not have a garlic press (see page 11), use the back of a knife or spoon against a cutting board, or a mortar and pestle, to mash garlic cloves.

- Avoid purchasing or using bulbs that are shriveled, yellow or moldy. They have a harsh taste.

- Rub cut cloves of garlic on a roast, and tuck whole cloves inside the meat before cooking, for a nice garlicky flavor.

- Rub cut cloves of garlic on bread (toasted or untoasted) and then spread lightly with olive oil.

- A new technique from the Gilroy Garlic Festival for roasting garlic is to place unpeeled garlic bulbs in a covered heavy skillet over medium-high heat, turning as each side becomes charred. The whole process takes about 15 minutes.

- Some schools of thought say to rub a salad bowl lightly with a cut clove of garlic. Others say that this is not a good idea if you are using a wooden bowl, as the garlic oils will eventually turn rancid.

- Garlic has been used to treat ill babies and children by various cultures for centuries. Recently, it has been shown that allicin, the substance in garlic that gives it its strong flavor, is similar to a European drug used to expel mucus and has been shown to be effective against colds.

- The Monell Chemical Senses Center in Philadelphia found that if mothers eat garlic at least 1 hour before breast feeding, it can help stimulate the baby's appetite. The study showed that the strong flavor and odor of garlic enticed the babies to nurse longer and consume more milk.
- Laboratory studies have shown that the sulfur compounds in garlic have anticoagulant (thinning) effects on the blood, preventing blood clots.
- Garlic has been linked to significantly lower rates of cancer in populations in China and Italy.

Whether your attraction to garlic is for reasons of healthy eating or creative cuisine, exploring the limitless possibilities of garlic cooking will be fun and satisfying. From mild and subtle to intense and robust, the following collection of easy-to-prepare and absolutely delicious garlic-enhanced recipes is sure to please you and your guests.

THE COOK'S TOOLS

GARLIC CELLAR/KEEPER

A covered container made of stoneware, terra cotta or porcelain. These storage pots provide the ideal environment for storing garlic. The small, back-to-back holes allow for just the right amount of light and ventilation to keep garlic fresh. Garlic cellars and keepers are available in a variety of shapes and sizes and are relatively inexpensive.

 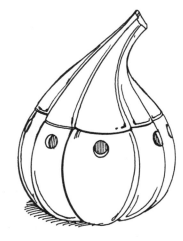

GARLIC BAKERS

A unique, easy-to-use kitchen accessory designed specifically for baking garlic. Baked garlic has less pungency and a much sweeter, subtler flavor. Season the garlic before baking and add it to seafood, poultry, meats and pasta dishes, or simply spread it on crackers or hot crusty breads. Garlic bakers are available in several styles and can accommodate from 1 to 5 bulbs.

GARLIC PRESS

A kitchen tool used to press a garlic clove through small holes, extracting pulp and juice. A top-quality garlic press is an indispensable kitchen tool. Don't bother with the inexpensive models. Purchase a sturdy metal press with a high extrusion rate. Most good garlic presses don't require the cloves to be peeled and are very easy to clean.

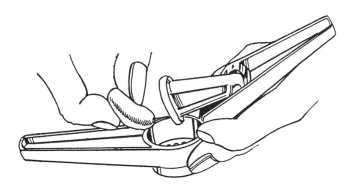

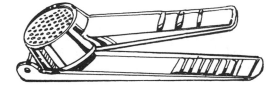

GARLIC SLICER/SHREDDER

A handy and innovative kitchen accessory that is ideal for cutting large quantities of garlic in uniform slices. It resembles a mandolin but is much smaller in size. Made with strong, sharp stainless steel blades, it has a well-designed holder for securing garlic cloves while protecting your fingers. The reversible blade is excellent for preparing fine shredded garlic.

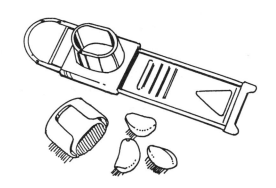

GARLIC CRUSHER/EXTRUDER

A see-through vertical garlic press with the added benefit of storing unused portions of garlic. To use, simply fill the cylinder with peeled garlic cloves. Twist the handle to release the amount of crushed garlic you need, and secure the cap on the bottom to store the remaining cloves. It stores the garlic odor-free and comes apart for easy cleaning.

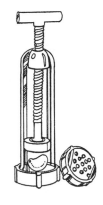

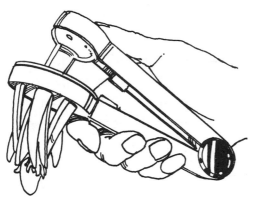

GARLIC PEELER

This is a technological breakthrough. Place 1 garlic clove in the peeler basket. Press the handle tightly, and a peeled clove of garlic falls through the bottom. It's ideal for peeling large quantities of garlic in a short period of time. It is easy to use and well constructed.

CRACK AND PEEL GARLIC OPENER

A mushroom-shaped hardwood gadget designed to crack open the skin on a clove of garlic. Just hold the comfortable handle in your palm to get a firm grip. Press down on 1 garlic clove, crack and remove the skin. Turn mushroom over and use the round side to crush herbs and spices in a small wooden bowl.

6- OR 8-INCH CHEF KNIFE

An indispensable kitchen tool for slicing, chopping and mincing garlic. The side of the blade can be used for peeling the cloves. Just press the flat side of the knife against the clove to loosen the skin. I recommend a strong, high-carbon stainless steel blade with a comfortable handle.

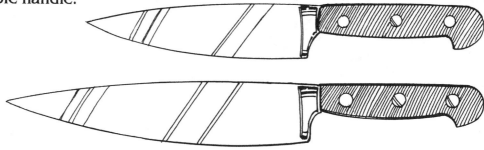

ODOR REMOVER

A small, 3-x-2-inch flat bar made from a metal alloy that completely washes away the garlic odor, which some people find offensive. Simply rub the bar over your hands under cool running water. The bar causes a reaction that releases the garlic oils from your skin. For best results, wash your hands as soon as possible. It also eliminates stubborn onion and fish odors.

APPETIZERS

BRUSCHETTA

This dish is delicious hot or cold. Be sure to use extra virgin olive oil and fresh tomatoes for a spirited flavor. Try substituting mozzarella cheese for the fontina.

6 slices wide country or Italian bread, 1 inch thick
1/3 cup extra virgin olive oil
4 cloves garlic, minced or squeezed through a press
2 cups diced tomatoes, 1/4-inch pieces
6 marinated artichoke hearts
1 cup grated fontina cheese
1/2 tsp. dried basil

Toast or grill both sides of bread. Combine olive oil and garlic in a small skillet and sauté over medium heat for 2 minutes. Generously brush one side of each slice of bread with garlic oil. Cover oiled bread with a layer of tomatoes. Top with artichoke hearts and cheese. Sprinkle with basil. Place on a baking sheet and bake in a preheated 400° oven for 10 minutes. Heat under the broiler for 2 minutes.

FRIED ARTICHOKE HEARTS

Servings: 4

Serve hot or cold as a tasty appetizer. Use unmarinated artichoke hearts for best results. For a variation, substitute 3-inch pieces of celery in place of the artichoke hearts.

1 can (14 oz.) unmarinated artichoke
  hearts
½ cup breadcrumbs
1 tbs. garlic powder
1 tbs. freshly grated Parmesan cheese

½ tsp. dried basil
½ tsp. dried parsley
1 tsp. freshly ground pepper
¼ cup olive oil
1 egg, beaten

Place artichoke hearts in a strainer and remove liquid. Slice artichoke hearts lengthwise into pieces 1 inch wide, 1½ inches long and ½-inch thick. In a shallow bowl, combine breadcrumbs, garlic powder, Parmesan cheese, basil, parsley and pepper. Mix thoroughly. Heat olive oil in a skillet. Dip each section of artichoke heart into egg and coat with breadcrumb mixture. Shake off excess. Sauté each piece for 2 to 3 minutes on each side, or until golden brown. Place on a paper towel-lined plate to absorb excess oil. Transfer to a serving plate.

ROASTED GARLIC CALZONE

Serve as a main course with a glass of wine, or cut into small pieces and serve as an appetizer for a crowd. You may prepare the dough in a bread machine, food processor, heavy-duty mixer or by hand.

1 bulb garlic, roasted (see page 64)
1 pkg. active dry yeast
1 cup plus 1 tbs. warm water
1 tbs. sugar
3¼ cups all-purpose flour

½ tsp. salt
2 tsp. dried basil
3 tbs. olive oil
2 cloves garlic, minced or squeezed
   through a press

Squeeze soft garlic from roasted cloves into a small bowl. Mash with a fork to form a paste and set aside.

To prepare dough: In a small bowl, dissolve yeast in water and add sugar. Set aside for 5 minutes. In a large bowl, combine flour, salt and basil. Mix well. Add yeast mixture, olive oil and minced or squeezed garlic to flour mixture. Stir together to form a ball. Place dough on a floured surface and knead for 10 minutes. Place dough in a greased bowl. Cover with a towel or plastic wrap and allow to rise for 1½ hours in a draft-free area. Punch down dough and allow to rest for 10 minutes.

FILLING

2 tbs. olive oil
1 cup sliced mushrooms
1 medium tomato, chopped
3 cups fresh spinach, firmly packed
1/2 cup shredded mozzarella cheese

1/2 cup shredded fontina cheese
2 tbs. chopped fresh basil
1/8 tsp. salt
1/4 tsp. freshly ground pepper

Heat 1 tbs. olive oil in a skillet and sauté mushrooms and tomato for 3 minutes. Add spinach and sauté for 2 to 3 minutes, or until spinach is wilted. Roll dough into a 15-inch circle. Brush half of dough with olive oil. Leaving a 1-inch border, spread roasted garlic paste evenly on oiled half of dough. Cover roasted garlic paste with a layer of mozzarella and fontina cheese. Cover cheese evenly with tomato-spinach mixture. Sprinkle fresh basil, salt and pepper on top of tomato-spinach mixture. Fold dough in half to evenly cover filling. Seal calzone by crimping edges of dough with your fingers. Carefully place calzone on a lightly oiled baking sheet. Brush top of calzone with olive oil. Bake in a preheated 500° oven for 20 minutes. Allow to cool for 15 minutes before serving. Serve hot or cold.

VARIATION

Top the tomato-spinach mixture with slices of prosciutto before baking.

GARLIC CHEESE SPREAD

Serve chilled as a dip or spread with fresh vegetables or crackers.

1 bulb garlic, roasted (see page 64)
4 oz. Gorgonzola cheese, cut into 1-inch pieces
8 oz. cream cheese, softened
1½ tsp. dried parsley
1½ tsp. dried basil

Squeeze soft garlic from roasted cloves. Combine garlic with remaining ingredients in a food processor or blender and process into a creamy spread. Transfer to a serving bowl and refrigerate for at least 2 hours, until ready to serve.

HUMMUS

A traditional Middle Eastern appetizer with a little zing. Try using a wooden lemon reamer to easily remove the juice and pulp from the lemons. Serve as a delicious dip with fresh pita bread slices or sliced carrots and other raw vegetables.

1 can (15 oz.) garbanzo beans
1/4 cup tahini (sesame seed paste)
2 tbs. water
1 tbs. olive oil
juice and pulp of 2 lemons, seeds removed
6 cloves garlic, squeezed through a press
1 tsp. chili powder
1/4 tsp. freshly ground pepper
1/8 tsp. salt
1/4 tsp. paprika

Drain liquid from garbanzo beans. Combine all ingredients, except paprika, in a food processor. Process for 4 minutes, or until smooth. Scoop into a serving bowl and sprinkle with paprika. Refrigerate for 2 hours. Serve chilled.

CHEESY GARLIC BREAD STICKS

Makes: 24

Serve these on your next antipasto or with a salad or pasta dish. If you prefer, use your bread machine, food processor or heavy-duty mixer to make the dough.

1 pkg. active dry yeast
1 cup plus 1 tbs. warm water
1 tbs. sugar
3¼ cups all-purpose flour
1 cup freshly grated Parmesan cheese, lightly packed
2 tsp. dried basil
½ tsp. salt
3 tbs. olive oil
2 cloves garlic, minced or squeezed through a press
2-3 tbs. cold water
1 tbs. garlic powder

In a small bowl, dissolve yeast in 1 cup warm water and add sugar. Set aside for 5 minutes. In a large bowl, combine flour, Parmesan cheese, basil and salt. Mix well. Add yeast mixture, olive oil and garlic to flour mixture. Stir together to form a ball. Place dough on a floured surface and knead for 10 minutes. Place dough in a greased bowl. Cover with a towel or plastic wrap and allow to rise for $1\frac{1}{2}$ hours in a draft-free area. Punch down dough and allow to rest for 10 minutes. Divide dough into 24 equal pieces. Roll out each piece and shape into an 8- to 10-inch-long stick. Place bread sticks on nonstick cookie sheets or on baking pans sprayed with nonstick cooking spray. Brush top of each bread stick with cold water and sprinkle with garlic powder. Bake in a preheated 400° oven for 20 minutes. Cool on a wire rack. Serve hot or cold.

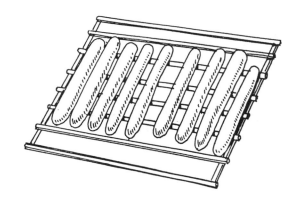

CRISPY GARLIC, CARROTS AND ZUCCHINI

Servings: 8

Here's a new and exciting way to prepare garlic, carrots and zucchini. The fried garlic slices release a subtle garlic flavor in the oil, which is absorbed by the other vegetables. Serve vegetables together as an appetizer or mix into salads.

8 medium carrots
2 medium zucchini
8 cloves garlic
1 cup olive or vegetable oil

Cut carrots and zucchini lengthwise into long, thin $\frac{1}{16}$-inch slices. Cut garlic cloves into $\frac{1}{16}$-inch-flat slices. Heat oil in a deep skillet. Sauté carrot, zucchini and garlic slices for 2 to 3 minutes, or until edges turn slightly brown and crisp. Place on a paper towel-lined plate to drain. Allow to cool and serve at room temperature.

GARLIC SALSA

*Your guests will rave about this appetizer and you'll have requests for more. Serve with **Garlic Pita Chips**, page 26, or as a topping for baked poultry or fish.*

6 cloves garlic, minced or squeezed through a press
1 can (1 lb. 12 oz.) crushed tomatoes in puree
¼ cup chopped fresh cilantro
¼ cup chopped scallions
1 tsp. fresh lime juice
2 tbs. chopped jalapeño peppers
1 tbs. chili powder

In a large bowl, combine all ingredients. Mix thoroughly and refrigerate for at least 2 hours.

GARLIC PITA CHIPS

*Delicious and addictive. I enjoy these served with cold **Garlic Salsa**, page 25, but they easily stand on their own and can be prepared a day in advance. Serve hot or cold as chips, or with a thin slice of Monterey Jack cheese.*

2 tbs. butter
½ cup olive oil
8 cloves garlic, squeezed through a press
6 loaves pita bread

Melt butter in a small saucepan. Add olive oil and garlic to melted butter and sauté over low heat for 10 minutes. Split open pita pockets and cut in half. Each pita will make 4 half-moon shapes. With rough side up, lay pita slices on a baking sheet. Brush entire surface with garlic mixture. Bake in a preheated 350° oven for 10 minutes. Place under the broiler for 1 minute, or until golden brown. Remove from oven and place on paper towels to absorb excess oil. Break into 2-inch pieces and serve in a large bowl or towel-lined wicker basket.

VARIATION

Sprinkle with dried basil or oregano before baking.

GARLIC-FLAVORED POPCORN

This is a dramatic twist to ordinary popcorn. It's simple to prepare and should be served immediately for maximum flavor.

3 tbs. butter
½ tsp. garlic powder
2 tbs. vegetable oil
½ cup high-quality popcorn kernels

Melt butter in a small saucepan. Add garlic powder and mix well. Heat oil in a 3½- to 4½-quart pot over medium-high heat for 20 seconds. Add popcorn kernels. Stir until all kernels are coated with oil. Cover pot. As soon as the first kernel pops, shake continuously until all kernels have popped. Remove from heat and empty popped kernels into a large bowl. Add melted garlic-butter and toss.

VARIATION

For a special treat, flavor popped kernels with ¾ cup finely grated cheddar cheese and place in a preheated 325° oven for 6 minutes.

GARLIC BREAD

Garlic bread was probably invented in the United States during the era of Italian-American restaurants in the late 1940s. Use Italian bread instead of French, if you prefer.

4 cloves garlic
1 loaf French bread
1/2 cup butter

Cut garlic cloves in half. Slice French bread loaf through center into 2 long, equally thick pieces. Place bread under the broiler. Lightly toast bread, carefully watching to avoid burning. Remove bread from oven and quickly rub crusty surface with cut garlic. Butter bread. Serve immediately, or reheat in the oven for 3 to 5 minutes before serving.

GARLIC HERB BUTTER

This butter is delicious on warm bread or rolls. Use it when cooking fish, lamb, vegetables or poultry. For an elegant flair, place the butter in the freezer for 20 minutes, and use a butter curler to scrape the top off the semi-frozen butter into sculptured swirls.

½ cup butter, or margarine
2 cloves garlic, squeezed through a press
½ tsp. dried basil
½ tsp. dried thyme

Soften butter. Combine all ingredients in a food processor or blend together in a small bowl with a fork or spoon. Keep refrigerated or freeze for future use.

VARIATION

Substitute spices with 1 tsp. dried tarragon or oregano. You can substitute ¼ tsp. garlic powder for the garlic cloves.

GARLIC HERB PIZZA

Servings: 6-8

This dough makes an incredibly delicious crust. Together it's the ultimate pizza. If you prefer, you can combine and knead the dough in a food processor, heavy-duty mixer or bread machine.

1 pkg. active dry yeast
1 cup plus 1 tbs. warm water
1 tbs. sugar
3¼ cups all-purpose flour
½ tsp. salt
2 tsp. dried basil
3 tbs. olive oil
2 cloves garlic, minced or squeezed through a press
¾ cup tomato pizza sauce
1 tomato, thinly sliced
2 cloves garlic, thinly sliced
¾ cup shredded mozzarella cheese
1 cup shredded Monterey Jack cheese
1 tbs. freshly grated Parmesan cheese
1 tsp. dried oregano

In a small bowl, dissolve yeast in water and add sugar. Set aside for 5 minutes. In a large bowl, combine flour, salt and basil and mix well. Add yeast mixture, olive oil and garlic to flour mixture. Stir together to form a ball. Place dough on a floured surface and knead for 10 minutes. Place dough in a greased bowl. Cover with a towel or plastic wrap and allow to rise for 1½ hours in a draft-free area. Punch down dough and allow to rest for 10 minutes. Roll out dough to fit a 14-inch pizza pan or ceramic baking stone. Spoon tomato sauce evenly over dough, leaving a 1-inch border around outside edge. Distribute tomato and garlic slices on sauce. Top with cheeses. Sprinkle with oregano. Bake in a preheated 425° oven for 25 minutes.

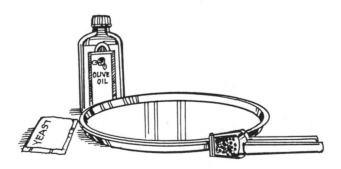

BAKED GARLIC AND HERB BREAD

Servings: 8-12

This incredibly delicious focaccia goes well with just about any dish. Use a food processor, heavy-duty mixer or bread machine, if desired.

1 pkg. active dry yeast
1 cup plus 1 tbs. warm water
1 tbs. sugar
3¼ cups all-purpose flour
½ tsp. salt
5 tbs. olive oil
2 cloves garlic, squeezed through a press
½ tsp. ground dried rosemary
½ tsp. dried basil

In a small bowl, dissolve yeast in water and add sugar. Set aside for 5 minutes. In a large bowl, combine flour and salt. Mix well. Add yeast mixture, 3 tbs. olive oil and garlic to flour mixture. Stir together to form a ball. Place dough on a floured surface and knead for 10 minutes. Place dough in a greased bowl. Cover with a towel or plastic wrap and allow to rise for 1½ hours in a draft-free area. Punch down dough and allow to rest for 10 minutes. Roll out dough to fit an 8½-x-12-inch baking pan. Brush bottom and sides of pan with olive oil. Place dough in pan, pressing and stretching so it extends to all sides of pan. Pierce top of dough with a fork about every 2 to 3 inches. Brush top of dough with olive oil. Sprinkle with rosemary and basil. Bake in a preheated 400° oven for 25 minutes. Brush top with remaining olive oil and broil for 3 to 5 minutes, or until top is golden brown. Serve hot or at room temperature.

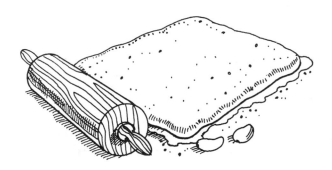

RIO RANCHERO SEAFOOD SALSA

*Serve with **Garlic Pita Chips**, page 26, as a topping for tacos or as a meal in itself — the fresh garlic and seafood come together beautifully for a spicy and nutritious meal.*

1 can (1 lb. 12 oz.) crushed tomato in puree
1 medium onion, finely chopped
6 cloves garlic, minced or squeezed through a press
2 tbs. chopped jalapeño peppers
1 tbs. chili powder
1 can (4.5 oz.) mild green chili peppers
1 tsp. finely chopped fresh cilantro
½ lb. cooked small shrimp, or large shrimp cut into bite-sized pieces
½ lb. cooked crabmeat, shredded into bite-sized pieces

In a large bowl, combine crushed tomato, onion, garlic, peppers, chili powder, chili peppers and cilantro. Mix thoroughly. Stir in shrimp and crabmeat. Cover bowl and refrigerate for at least 2 hours. Serve chilled.

ROASTED GARLIC AND BROCCOLI CHEESE SPREAD

The roasted garlic adds a rich and delicious flavor to the spread without any added fat. Make this ahead of time. A perfect dip for a casual party setting. Serve with crackers or fresh vegetables.

4 cloves garlic, roasted (see page 64)
½ lb. broccoli florets and stems
8 oz. cream cheese
2 tsp. chives

Remove skin or squeeze soft garlic from roasted cloves and set aside. Cook broccoli in a steamer for 3 to 4 minutes, or until bright green. Set aside and allow to cool. Combine broccoli, garlic, cream cheese and chives in a food processor. Process until mixture is smooth. Remove from food processor and chill for 2½ hours.

TEX-MEX GARLIC PIZZA

Spicy and flavorful, this alternative to the traditional Italian tomato-sauced pizza makes a great appetizer or side dish. Bread machines, food processors and heavy-duty mixers stand in for hand-kneading.

1 pkg. active dry yeast
1 cup plus 1 tbs. warm water
1 tbs. sugar
$3\frac{1}{4}$ cups all-purpose flour
$\frac{1}{2}$ tsp. salt
5 tbs. olive oil
8 cloves garlic, minced
$\frac{3}{4}$ cup shredded mozzarella cheese
$\frac{3}{4}$ cup shredded Monterey Jack cheese
$\frac{3}{4}$ cup grated Parmesan cheese
2 tsp. dried jalapeño flakes, reconstituted, or 4
  jalapeño peppers, seeded and finely chopped
1 tsp. dried red pepper flakes
$\frac{1}{2}$ tsp. chili powder

In a small bowl, dissolve yeast in warm water and add sugar. Set aside for 5 minutes. In a large bowl, combine flour and salt. Mix well. Add yeast mixture, 3 tbs. olive oil and 2 minced garlic cloves to flour mixture. Stir together to form a ball. Place dough on a floured surface and knead for 10 minutes. Place dough in a greased bowl. Cover with a towel or plastic wrap and allow to rise for 1½ hours in a draft-free area. Punch down dough and allow to rest for 10 minutes. Brush a 14-inch pizza pan with olive oil and roll out dough to fit pan. Brush dough with olive oil. Top with cheeses. Sprinkle with remaining garlic, jalapeño flakes, red pepper flakes and chili powder. Bake in a preheated 425° oven for 25 to 30 minutes, or until cheese starts to bubble and turn golden brown.

ROASTED GARLIC PASTRY PUFFS

Makes: 36

Serve these at your next party. They'll be a sure hit. The crust is delicious, the filling is incredible and the garlic flavor is somewhat indistinguishable.

FILLING

2 bulbs garlic, roasted (see page 64)
4 tbs. butter
$\frac{1}{2}$ cup finely chopped celery
1 cup finely chopped onions
$3\frac{1}{2}$ cups finely chopped mushrooms
$\frac{1}{2}$ tsp. dried thyme

PASTRY

$\frac{1}{4}$ cup butter, softened
$\frac{3}{4}$ cup shredded cheddar cheese
$\frac{1}{4}$ cup shredded Monterey Jack cheese
1 cup flour
2 tbs. water

To prepare filling: Separate roasted garlic cloves, peel and mash together to form a paste. Melt butter in a skillet. Add celery and onions. Sauté on medium heat for 5 minutes. Add garlic paste and sauté for 4 minutes. Add mushrooms and thyme; sauté for 6 minutes. Set aside and allow to cool.

To prepare pastry: In a medium bowl, cream together butter and cheeses. Blend flour into mixture. Starting with 1 tbs., add water as needed to form dough.

Roll dough into thin sheets and cut into 4-x-4-inch squares. Place a teaspoon of filling on a corner, covering about half of the square, at an angle. Fold over other half of dough to form a triangle. Crimp edges to seal. Place pastry puffs on a nonstick or lightly greased cookie sheet. Bake in a preheated 400° oven for 20 minutes, or until golden brown. Allow to cool and serve at room temperature.

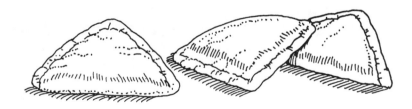

SOUPS AND SALADS

GARLIC ONION SOUP

Serve as a first course or as an accompaniment to a fresh salad or sandwich.

1 bulb garlic, roasted (see page 64)
3 tbs. butter
5 medium onions, thinly sliced
1 can (13¾ oz.) beef broth

7 cups water
4 beef bouillon cubes
1 tbs. Worcestershire sauce
Garlic Croutons, page 45

Squeeze roasted garlic from each clove and set aside. Melt butter in a skillet. Add onion slices and sauté over medium-low heat for 30 minutes. Do not cover skillet. In a large saucepan or stockpot, combine beef broth, water, bouillon cubes, Worcestershire sauce and roasted garlic. Simmer for 30 minutes. Remove broth mixture from heat and allow to cool; pour into a food processor or blender and puree. Depending on the size of your food processor, you may have to process this in two or three batches. Return pureed mixture to stockpot. Add sautéed onions and simmer for 30 minutes. Serve in individual soup bowls with *Garlic Croutons*.

GAZPACHO

A refreshing summertime soup. This soup is excellent served with **Garlic Croutons***, page 45.*

3 cloves garlic, minced or squeezed through a press
1 lb. tomatoes, peeled and chopped
1 medium cucumber, peeled and chopped
1 large red bell pepper, seeded, cored and chopped
3 medium onions, chopped
1 tbs. plus 1½ tsp. olive oil
1 tbs. plus 1½ tsp. red wine vinegar
1½ cup tomato juice
1 tsp. sugar
½ tsp. salt
½ tsp. freshly ground pepper

Combine all ingredients in a large bowl and mix thoroughly. Pour batches of mixture into a food processor or blender and process until almost a puree. The soup should have texture, so do not overprocess. Transfer soup to a large bowl and refrigerate for 2 hours, or overnight. Serve cold in chilled individual bowls.

TOMATO SLICES WITH BASIL AND GARLIC

A traditional Italian favorite. Use only vine-ripened, fresh tomatoes. Serve as a salad or on a platter for a buffet.

6 medium tomatoes
¼ head lettuce
2 cloves garlic, minced or
   squeezed through a press
2 tbs. minced fresh basil
½ tsp. freshly ground pepper
4 tbs. light extra virgin olive oil

Cut tomatoes into ¼-inch slices. Line a platter or small individual plates with fresh lettuce. Arrange a layer of tomato slices on top of lettuce. Combine garlic, basil, pepper and olive oil and sprinkle over tomato slices. Refrigerate for 1 hour before serving.

CAESAR SALAD

A shallow wooden bowl made of hard rock maple is ideal for preparing and presenting this salad.

1 small or ½ large head romaine lettuce
2 cloves garlic
3 tbs. extra virgin olive oil
1 clove garlic, sliced in half, optional
1 tbs. fresh lemon juice

⅛ tsp. freshly ground pepper
⅛ tsp. salt
2 flat anchovy fillets, chopped
½ cup *Garlic Croutons*, page 45
1 tbs. freshly grated Parmesan cheese

Carefully wash lettuce, tear into large pieces and set aside. Combine 2 cloves garlic and olive oil in a food processor or blender and process until smooth. Rub entire inner surface of a wooden salad bowl with cut garlic, if desired. Pour garlic-oil mixture into a small bowl. Add lemon juice, pepper, salt and anchovies. Blend ingredients together. Place lettuce in salad bowl, pour on dressing and *Garlic Croutons*, and toss thoroughly. Sprinkle with freshly grated Parmesan cheese. Serve immediately.

GARLIC CROUTONS

Serve with soups or salads for a spicy treat. This is a clever way to use up stale bread.

3 cups (about 6 slices) day-old Italian bread,
    crusts removed, cut into ¾-inch cubes
4 tbs. unsalted butter
3 cloves garlic, minced or squeezed through a press
½ tsp. dried basil
½ tsp. dried parsley

Prepare bread cubes and set aside. Melt butter in a nonstick skillet over medium heat. Add garlic, basil and parsley. Add bread, reduce heat to medium-low and sauté for 4 to 5 minutes. Stir constantly. Remove from heat and place croutons on baking sheets. Bake in a preheated 325° oven for 25 minutes, or until golden brown. Stir occasionally.

VEGETARIAN SALAD

In place of ordinary table salt, use sea salt. It's produced from the evaporation of sea water and contains natural iodine, an essential nutrient. This salad is delicious and filling. Lentils are an often neglected legume that taste great in salads, soups and hot side dishes.

$\frac{1}{2}$ cup lentils
$\frac{1}{4}$ cup olive oil
8 cloves garlic, minced or squeezed through a press
$\frac{1}{4}$ cup chopped red onion
$\frac{1}{2}$ cup chopped red bell pepper
$\frac{1}{3}$ cup chopped celery
$\frac{1}{3}$ cup sliced fresh mushrooms
$\frac{1}{2}$ cup chopped tomatoes
1 tbs. fresh oregano, or 1 tsp. dried
$1\frac{1}{2}$ tsp. fresh mint, or $\frac{1}{2}$ tsp. dried
$\frac{1}{4}$ tsp. freshly ground pepper
$\frac{1}{8}$ tsp. sea salt

Rinse lentils under cold water. Bring lentils to a boil in water, reduce heat and simmer for 40 minutes. Drain and set aside. Heat ¼ cup olive oil in a large skillet. Add garlic and onion and sauté over low heat for 4 minutes. Add red peppers, celery and mushrooms. Cook over medium-low heat for about 5 minutes, or until vegetables are soft. Add lentils, tomatoes, oregano, mint, pepper and salt. Cover and simmer for 3 minutes, stirring occasionally. Serve hot or cold.

VARIATION

Add 1 cup tomato sauce and serve as a tomato-based side dish or over pasta.

TABOULI

This Middle Eastern salad comes together beautifully. The parsley and lemon bring out the wonderful flavors of all the vegetables and spices. Arrange a sampling of tabouli on a large platter with fresh leafy greens, hummus, marinated olives and grilled pita wedges for an attractive and delicious Mediterranean antipasto. Serve with fresh pita bread.

½ cup bulghur wheat
1 cup water
2 cups chopped fresh parsley, firmly packed
1 small cucumber, finely chopped
1 large tomato, finely chopped
3 medium red onions, finely chopped
2 tbs. finely chopped fresh mint
¼ tsp. freshly ground pepper
2 cloves garlic, minced or squeezed through a press
¼ cup (about 1½ lemons) fresh lemon juice
1 tbs. olive or canola oil

Combine bulghur wheat and water and soak for 2 hours. In a large bowl, combine parsley, cucumber, tomato, onions, mint and pepper. Mix thoroughly. Drain bulghur and combine with vegetables and spices. Add garlic and lemon juice. Slowly stir in oil. Mix and refrigerate for at least 3 hours before serving.

RED RASPBERRY AND GARLIC VINAIGRETTE

This delicious, low fat dressing is good for any salad. It's also a wonderful marinade for poultry and seafood. For gift-giving, try dripping hot candle wax over the bottle corks to enforce the tight seal and add a decorative touch.

6 tbs. *Red Raspberry Vinegar*, follows
2 tbs. olive oil
2 cloves garlic, squeezed through a press
2 tsp. minced fresh basil
1 tsp. Dijon mustard

Combine all ingredients in a bowl or bottle and mix together vigorously. Store in an air-tight container and shake well before using.

RED RASPBERRY VINEGAR

2 cups (16 oz.) white wine vinegar
¼ cup clover honey
¼ cup blueberries, fresh, or frozen, thawed
½ cup red raspberries, fresh, or frozen, thawed
½ cup cranberries, fresh, or frozen, thawed
2 cinnamon sticks, each 2 inches long
2 whole cloves

Bring vinegar to a low boil in a saucepan. Reduce heat to simmer. Add honey, blueberries, ¼ cup raspberries and ¼ cup cranberries. Allow to cool for 1 hour. Strain through a very fine mesh stainless steel strainer or cheesecloth. Pour vinegar into old sterilized wine bottles or decorative glass jars. Add remaining berries and spices. Seal glass containers with tight-fitting corks and store in a dark, dry area for 2 weeks.

GARLICKY VINAIGRETTE

Pour over or toss with a fresh garden salad or cold pasta salad. Also works great as a marinade for meats, poultry, fish or vegetables. Make a fresh batch of vinaigrette each time. Do not store for longer than a day or two.

3 tbs. balsamic vinegar
¾ cup extra virgin olive oil
¼ tsp. freshly ground pepper
2 cloves garlic, minced or squeezed through a press
2 tsp. chopped fresh basil
1 tbs. fresh lemon juice

In a medium bowl, combine all ingredients and whisk together until evenly blended.

TOMATO GARLIC VINAIGRETTE DRESSING

This is delicious over leafy greens, tomatoes and cucumbers. Mustard lovers can add 1 tbs. Dijon mustard to ingredients for extra flavor.

1 cup tomato juice
2 cloves garlic, minced or squeezed through a press
3 tbs. balsamic vinegar
4 tbs. extra virgin olive oil
$\frac{1}{8}$ tsp. dried basil
$\frac{1}{8}$ tsp. dried parsley
$\frac{1}{8}$ tsp. freshly ground pepper

Combine all ingredients in a medium bowl and blend together with a wire whisk. Store in the refrigerator.

GARLIC VINEGAR

For a subtle garlic flavor, use this in place of regular vinegar in vinaigrettes and sauces.

5 cloves garlic, minced or squeezed through a press
12 oz. white or red wine vinegar

Combine garlic and vinegar in a clear glass bottle. Carefully seal bottle and allow to sit for 2 weeks in a well-lighted area, such as a kitchen counter. Strain garlic pieces from vinegar. Store flavored vinegar in a cool, dark area.

BASIC GARLIC SALAD DRESSING AND MARINADE

Serve on antipasto or on a fresh garden salad. This is also an excellent and easy-to-prepare marinade for meats.

1/4 cup extra virgin olive oil
2 tbs. white or red wine vinegar
2 cloves garlic, minced or squeezed through a press
1/4 tsp. freshly ground pepper
salt to taste

Combine all ingredients in a small bowl and mix together thoroughly.

GARLIC MAYONNAISE

Makes: about ¾ cup

To mix ingredients together, use a sturdy stainless steel whisk with a comfortable handle. If you're using a food processor or blender, be sure to add the ingredients in the correct order.

1 egg yolk
½ tsp. Dijon mustard
¼ tsp. salt
2 cloves garlic, squeezed through a press
¾ cup olive oil
1 tbs. fresh lemon juice

All ingredients should be at room temperature. In a small bowl, combine egg yolk, mustard, salt and garlic. Whisk together continuously. Slowly add olive oil, a drop at a time, building up to a slow stream. After all olive oil has been blended into mixture, whisk in lemon juice. Keep mayonnaise refrigerated in a glass jar with a tight seal.

GARLIC AND HONEY SALAD DRESSING

Enhance the flavor of a well-made salad with this interesting dressing.

2 tbs. white or red wine vinegar
$\frac{1}{4}$ tsp. sea salt
$\frac{1}{4}$ tsp. freshly ground pepper
1 clove garlic, minced or squeezed through a press
$\frac{1}{2}$ tsp. Dijon mustard
1 tsp. honey
$\frac{1}{3}$ cup extra virgin olive oil
1 tbs. chopped fresh basil

Combine vinegar, salt, pepper, garlic, mustard and honey in a small bowl. Mix thoroughly. Slowly add olive oil, stirring constantly. Add basil and blend. Store in an airtight container. Shake before using.

GARLIC-LEMON PEPPERCORNS

Invest in a high-quality pepper mill. Freshly ground pepper will enhance the flavors of your foods. This flavored pepper adds a zesty sparkle to seafoods, poultry and vegetables.

3 tbs. cracked black peppercorns
2¼ tsp. dried minced garlic
1 tsp. dried lemon peel

Mix all ingredients together and grind in a pepper mill or with a mortar and pestle.

ITALIAN SEASONINGS

Making your own Italian seasonings is easy and adds a great flavor to beef, poultry, seafood, vegetables and sauces.

¼ tsp. dried minced garlic
⅛ tsp. dried red pepper flakes
½ tsp. dried rosemary
1 tsp. dried basil

1 tsp. dried oregano
½ tsp. dried marjoram
½ tsp. dried thyme

Grind garlic, red pepper flakes and rosemary in a spice mill or with a mortar and pestle. Combine all ingredients and mix thoroughly. Store in an airtight glass jar. Keep out of direct sunlight.

TORTELLINI SALAD

This tantalizing vinaigrette melds the flavors of the vegetables and pasta beautifully. For best results, use fresh, crisp, colorful farm stand vegetables.

1 pkg. (14 oz.) fresh or frozen cheese tortellini
1 cup snow peas
4 cups broccoli florets and sliced stems
1 medium red or green bell pepper, cut into ½-inch pieces
3 plum tomatoes, chopped
½ cup marinated artichokes hearts, drained and quartered
⅛ tsp. sea salt
2-4 oz. *Red Raspberry and Garlic Vinaigrette*, page 50

Cook tortellini in a large pot, according to package instructions. Rinse under cold water and drain thoroughly. Snip off ends of pea pods. Steam or boil broccoli for 5 minutes and peas for 1 minute; quickly drain and place in ice cold water for 2 to 3 minutes. In a large bowl, combine tortellini, broccoli, peas, pepper, tomatoes, artichoke hearts and salt. Mix thoroughly. Toss with *Red Raspberry and Garlic Vinaigrette*.

PASTA VEGETABLE SALAD

A light and tasty dish that's especially delicious on warm summer days — but good anytime.

2-4 oz. *Garlicky Vinaigrette*, page 52
16 oz. dried tri-colored pasta shells or spirals
1 medium red onion, finely chopped
1 red or green bell pepper, finely chopped
2 large carrots, sliced into $\frac{1}{8}$-inch rounds
2 stalks celery, chopped
$\frac{1}{8}$ tsp. sea salt

Prepare *Garlicky Vinaigrette*. Cook pasta according to package instructions. Rinse under cold water and drain well. In a large bowl, toss pasta with vegetables, salt and *Garlicky Vinaigrette*. Refrigerate and serve cold.

VEGETABLES AND SIDE DISHES

ROASTED GARLIC

Roasting garlic mellows its pungency and produces a delicious sweet flavor. I strongly recommend a terra cotta garlic baker with a large diameter so you can roast several bulbs at a time or large elephant garlic bulbs. Serve roasted garlic warm as a spread, or use in other recipes. Increase the recipe size as needed.

1 large bulb garlic
1/4 tsp. or 1 tbs. olive oil (see method)
1 tsp. butter, optional
1/8 tsp. dried basil
1/8 tsp. dried thyme
freshly ground pepper to taste

For perfectly roasted garlic, cut 1/4 inch off top of garlic bulb. Remove loose outer leaves. Bulb should remain intact. Pour 1/4 tsp. olive oil over bulb and dot with butter, or pour 1 tbs. olive oil over bulb and eliminate butter. Sprinkle with basil, thyme and pepper. Place cover on garlic baker. For a medium to large bulb, bake in a preheated 350° oven for 50 minutes. For an extra large bulb, bake for an additional 10 minutes. If cooking in a microwave oven, prepare bulb as directed and cook on HIGH for 1½ minutes. Separate cloves and squeeze out garlic.

AUTHENTIC ROASTED PEPPERS

Servings: 8

Commercially prepared or boiled, skinned roasted peppers just don't compare. These are absolutely addictive. Use large thick bell peppers. You can roast the peppers under a broiler or on an outdoor grill. Removing the seeds and stems before roasting makes preparing this dish much easier.

8 large red or green bell peppers
7 cloves garlic, minced or squeezed through a press
1 cup olive oil

Leave peppers whole, but cut off tops and remove stems, membranes and all seeds. Rinse under cold water and drain. Place peppers on the grate of a hot grill or under a broiler. With metal tongs, turn peppers every 2 to 3 minutes. Peppers should be charred and blistered in 10 to 12 minutes. Place charred peppers in a brown paper bag. Place filled bag on a platter to prevent wet peppers from breaking through bag. Allow peppers to sit for at least 1 hour, or up to 1 day. Remove peppers from bag. Use your hands and easily peel off blistered skins. Discard skins. Slice peppers into 1½-inch strips and combine with garlic and olive oil. Refrigerate for at least 2 hours. Serve cold.

STUFFED ONIONS WITH ROASTED GARLIC

An absolutely delightful treat, these are incredibly delicious with any main course.

1 bulb garlic, roasted (see page 64)
4 large white onions
3 tbs. butter
2 stalks celery, finely chopped
1 cup seasoned breadcrumbs
½ tsp. dried basil

¼ tsp. dried thyme
½ tsp. dried parsley
¼ tsp. salt
¼ tsp. freshly ground pepper
3 tbs. grated Parmesan cheese
3 tbs. dry sherry

Separate roasted garlic cloves, peel and mash in a small bowl to form a paste. Set aside. Peel onions and cut off ends. Place onions in a 2½- to 3½-quart pot of boiling water for 25 minutes. Remove from pot and allow to cool for 15 minutes. Cut onions in half across the middle and remove cores, leaving outer 3 to 4 layers of onion intact. Insert a piece of onion core on end of each onion to cover up hole. Mince remaining onion cores (about ¼ cup) and reserve for stuffing.

To prepare stuffing: Melt butter in a skillet. Add celery and sauté for 5 to 7 minutes, or until tender. Add ¼ cup reserved onion and garlic paste and sauté for 4 minutes. Add breadcrumbs, basil, thyme, parsley, salt, pepper, Parmesan cheese and sherry.

Mix thoroughly and sauté on medium heat for 4 minutes.

Place hollowed onions in an ovenproof casserole. Fill centers with stuffing. Bake uncovered in a preheated 400° oven for 30 minutes.

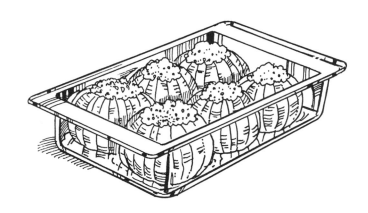

HEAVENLY RICE AND SPINACH

Leave standard potatoes or plain cooked rice behind! This adventurous side dish has an extraordinary rich flavor.

1/8 cup toasted pine nuts, optional
1 1/2 cups long grain white rice
5 tbs. butter
6 cloves garlic, minced or squeezed
   through a press
2 medium onions, finely chopped

1/4 tsp. salt
1/4 tsp. freshly ground pepper
4 cups chopped fresh spinach, firmly
   packed
3/4 cup chicken stock
1/2 cup freshly grated Parmesan cheese

Roast pine nuts in a dry skillet over medium heat, stirring constantly until seeds are golden brown. Set aside. Prepare rice according to package instructions. Melt butter in a large skillet. Add garlic and onions; sauté for 5 minutes. Add salt, pepper and spinach; sauté for 3 minutes, or until spinach becomes limp. Add chicken stock and cooked rice. Sauté for 5 minutes, or until rice is steaming hot. Stir in Parmesan cheese and toasted pine nuts. Remove from heat. Keep covered and serve warm.

STUFFED BAKED POTATOES

The roasted garlic stuffing blends very nicely with the Parmesan cheese for a perfectly flavored potato.

8 cloves garlic, roasted (see page 64)
4 large baking potatoes
2 tsp. minced fresh or freeze-dried
  chives

½ cup milk
4 tbs. butter, melted
3 tbs. grated Parmesan cheese

Separate roasted garlic cloves, peel and mash in a small bowl to form a paste. Set aside. Carefully scrub potatoes under cold running water with a high-quality vegetable brush to remove dirt. Place potatoes on an oven rack in a preheated 450° oven for 50 minutes. Slice potatoes in half, lengthwise, into 2 equal pieces. Carefully scoop out pulp without breaking skins. Mash or press pulp through a vegetable ricer. In a medium bowl, combine pulp with garlic, chives, milk, melted butter and 1 tbs. Parmesan cheese. Mix well. Refill potato skins with stuffing. Place potatoes on an ovenproof dish, and sprinkle tops with 2 tbs. Parmesan cheese. Bake in a preheated 400° oven for 10 minutes. Place under the broiler for 4 minutes, or until golden brown. Serve immediately.

ROASTED GARLIC AND SPINACH QUICHE

Servings: 6

To assure a perfect texture, carefully drain cooked spinach of all water.

1 bulb garlic, roasted (see page 64)
1 tbs. butter
1 small onion, finely chopped
4 eggs
1 cup milk
1/4 tsp. chili powder

1/2 tsp. salt
1/4 tsp. freshly ground pepper
1 cup cooked spinach, fresh or frozen,
  drained well
1/2 cup shredded Monterey Jack cheese
1/4 tsp. vegetable oil for oiling pan

Separate roasted garlic cloves, peel and mash in a small bowl to form a paste. Melt butter in a skillet. Add onion and sauté until soft, about 6 minutes. Add garlic paste and sauté for 4 minutes. Blend together and set aside. In a medium bowl, whisk together eggs, milk, chili powder, salt and pepper. In another bowl, combine garlic-onion mixture with spinach and cheese. Mix well. Spread spinach mixture firmly in a lightly oiled 9-inch quiche or pie pan. Pour egg mixture evenly over spinach. Bake in a preheated 350° oven for 40 minutes. Quiche is done when a toothpick inserted into the center comes out clean.

MARINARA SAUCE

This appetizing sauce is delicious with pasta and other cooked foods.

2 tbs. olive oil
3 cloves garlic, minced or squeezed through a press
1 medium onion, finely chopped
2 cans (28 oz. each) Italian plum tomatoes, chopped and mashed
$\frac{1}{2}$ tsp. dried oregano
2 tbs. chopped fresh basil
$\frac{1}{4}$ tsp. freshly ground pepper
$\frac{1}{8}$ tsp. salt

Heat olive oil in a medium saucepan over medium heat. Add garlic and onion and sauté for 5 to 7 minutes, or until onions are soft. Add tomatoes. Stir in oregano, basil, pepper and salt. Partially cover saucepan. Reduce heat and simmer for $1\frac{1}{2}$ hours. Stir occasionally.

ROASTED GARLIC BREAD

Servings: 8

This side dish is well worth the effort. Roasted garlic and a stick of freshly baked bread are just meant to be eaten together. The flavor is one that everyone enjoys.

2 bulbs garlic, roasted (see page 64)
1 tbs. olive oil
2 tbs. freshly grated Parmesan cheese
½ tsp. dried basil
¼ tsp. dried oregano
¼ tsp. dried parsley
¼ tsp. freshly ground pepper
1 loaf Italian bread or French baguette

Separate roasted garlic cloves, peel and mash in a small bowl to form a paste. Combine garlic paste with all remaining ingredients, except bread. Mix thoroughly. Slice bread in half lengthwise, separating top from bottom. Spread garlic mixture on inside of each half. Wrap each half in parchment paper or foil and bake in a preheated 350° oven for 10 minutes. Remove parchment paper or foil wrap from bread and place under the broiler for 2 to 3 minutes.

VARIATION

Slice bread at an angle, ³⁄₄ through, at 1-inch intervals. Spread garlic mixture between bread slices. Wrap bread and bake in a preheated 350° oven for 20 minutes. Serve warm.

GARLIC ROASTED POTATOES

Servings: 4

You can prepare these irresistible potatoes for any occasion. I recommend using medium-sized freezer bags for coating the potatoes with the seasonings.

1½ lb. new red-skinned potatoes
¼ cup olive oil
4 large cloves garlic, minced or squeezed through a press
½ tsp. dried basil
½ tsp. dried oregano
¼ tsp. freshly ground pepper

Wash potatoes under cold running water with a high-quality vegetable brush. Remove eyes, but do not peel. Cut into 1-inch cubes. In a medium-sized plastic bag, combine all ingredients. Shake until potatoes are evenly coated. Place potatoes in a single layer in an ovenproof baking dish. Bake for 50 minutes in a preheated 425° oven. Turn occasionally.

MARINATED MUSHROOMS

Always buy fresh mushrooms and use them within 3 days.

36 mushrooms
1 can (14.5 oz.) stewed tomatoes,
　chopped, with juice
½ cup dry sherry
⅓ cup olive oil
2 tbs. balsamic vinegar
¼ tsp. freshly ground pepper
6 cloves garlic, minced or squeezed
　through a press
juice of ½ lemon
2 tsp. dried oregano

Clean mushrooms with a damp cloth or a mushroom brush with soft bristles. If you wash mushrooms, use cold water and allow them to sit on paper towels to dry. Combine remaining ingredients in a large bowl and mix thoroughly. Add mushrooms. Cover with a tight seal and place in the refrigerator for 1 to 2 days. Stir occasionally.

FRESH VEGETABLE AND GARLIC MEDLEY

Servings: 4

This dish proves that you can have delicious food that is also good for you!

4 cloves garlic, thinly sliced
3 large carrots, peeled, cut into matchstick strips
1 medium zucchini, cut into matchstick strips
1 medium tomato, diced
1 medium red bell pepper, cut into matchstick strips
1 tbs. chopped fresh basil
½ tsp. freshly ground pepper
2 tbs. low sodium soy sauce

Combine all ingredients in a large bowl. Marinate in the refrigerator for 2 hours. Lay out two 18-x-15-inch sheets of parchment paper and fold in half. Open sheets of parchment paper and place half the ingredients on one side of each sheet, next to the fold. Fold and tightly seal packets by overlapping small ¼-inch folds or a series of long, thin folds along the sides. Place packets on a baking sheet and bake in a preheated 375° oven for 20 minutes. Transfer cooked vegetables to a large serving bowl or individual plates.

GRILLED ZUCCHINI

Serve as a vegetable side dish or as a main course with a marinara sauce and pasta.

16 oz. *Garlicky Vinaigrette*, page 52
8 tender young zucchini

Prepare *Garlicky Vinaigrette*. Slice zucchini in half lengthwise into 2 thick pieces. Place zucchini in a shallow bowl and cover with marinade. Cover and refrigerate for 4 hours, turning occasionally in marinade. Cook on a barbecue grill rack over medium-high heat for 10 to 12 minutes on each side, basting frequently with marinade, or cook under a broiler for 6 to 7 minutes on each side.

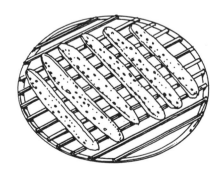

FRESH SPINACH WITH GARLIC

Spinach goes great with garlic. But spinach does not store very well. Buy it fresh and cook it within two days. A perfect accompaniment for a seafood dish.

¾ lb. fresh spinach, washed
⅓ cup olive oil
4 cloves garlic, thinly sliced
½ tsp. dried basil
½ tsp. freshly ground pepper

Wash spinach very thoroughly under cold running water. Be sure to remove all the grit. Cut out tough stems and leave spinach whole or break into large pieces. Place spinach in a medium saucepan in 1 inch water. Pour olive oil over spinach. Mix in garlic slices and sprinkle with basil and pepper. Bring to a boil. Cover, reduce heat to medium and cook for 5 to 7 minutes, or until tender. Serve in individual serving bowls with garlic-flavored liquid.

HARVEST SUN-MIXED VEGETABLES

The secret to this recipe is the fennel. It adds a delicious licorice flavor to the dish. It looks like celery and in some regions it is mislabeled as sweet anise.

2 tbs. canola or olive oil
4 cloves garlic, minced or squeezed
   through a press
1 medium onion, thinly sliced
1 bulb fennel, thinly sliced
1 medium zucchini, cut into $\frac{1}{4}$-inch
   rounds

1 medium red bell pepper, cut into
   1-inch pieces
2 cups broccoli florets and sliced stems
4 tbs. water
$\frac{1}{2}$ tsp. dried thyme
1 tsp. freshly ground pepper
juice of $\frac{1}{2}$ lemon

Heat oil in a deep skillet over low-medium heat. Add garlic and onion; sauté for 4 minutes. Add fennel, cover and cook for 5 minutes. Add zucchini, red pepper, broccoli, water, thyme and pepper. Cover and cook over medium heat for 10 to 12 minutes. Place cooked vegetables in a large serving bowl or on individual serving plates. Drizzle with lemon juice and serve immediately.

STEAMED ARTICHOKES
WITH GARLIC STUFFING

Carefully inspect the artichokes for quality. Look for clean, unblemished leaves and watch out for rotten spots. I prefer Italian or country-style bread for the stuffing, but you can substitute other varieties.

4 medium artichokes
8 slices day-old Italian or country-style bread, 1 inch thick
2 cloves garlic, minced or squeezed through a press
1/4 tsp. dried basil
1/2 cup olive oil
1/4 tsp. freshly ground pepper
2 tbs. grated Parmesan cheese

Remove 1 inch from artichoke stems. Discard tough bottom leaves. Slice off top 1/2 inch of each artichoke. Use kitchen shears to snip off points on all outer leaves, about 1/4 inch. To prepare artichokes for stuffing, open space between leaves by banging artichoke tops on the counter, or stretch open area between layers of leaves. Rinse artichokes under cold running water. Drain upside down and set aside.

To prepare stuffing: Cut bread, without crust, into 1-inch cubes. In a large bowl, combine bread, garlic, basil, olive oil, pepper and Parmesan cheese. Use clean hands to mix thoroughly. Starting with the second row of outer leaves, put a small amount of stuffing inside each leaf. Approximately 2 slices bread should fill each artichoke.

Place artichokes in an upright position in a large pot with 1 inch water. Bring water to a boil, cover and reduce heat to low. Cook for 35 to 45 minutes. To test if artichokes are cooked sufficiently, use a tong and pull on outer leaves. When leaves are removed easily, artichokes are done. Serve hot or cold in individual plates as an appetizer or first course.

POTATO FANTASY

A new-style potato side dish, this goes especially well with lamb or beef.

2 tbs. flour
8 medium new potatoes
2 tbs. butter
2 tbs. olive oil
4 cloves garlic, minced or squeezed through a press
½ cup chopped scallions
2 celery stalks, finely chopped
1 cup thinly sliced mushrooms
¾ cup chicken broth
3 tbs. chopped fresh basil
2 tsp. honey
1½ tsp. *Italian Seasonings*, page 59
⅛ tsp. salt
fresh parsley for garnish

Brown flour in a dry skillet over medium heat, stirring occasionally, for 8 minutes and set aside. Boil potatoes for 18 minutes, or until tender. Drain and submerge potatoes in cold water. Slice or cube potatoes and set aside. Heat butter and olive oil in a deep skillet. Sauté garlic for 2 minutes over medium heat. Add scallions, celery and mushrooms. Sauté for 3 minutes. Add chicken broth, basil, honey, *Italian Seasonings* and salt. As soon as liquid begins to boil, slowly whisk in flour. Add potatoes and simmer for 3 to 5 minutes, or until potatoes are warm. Mix thoroughly and serve at room temperature with sprigs of fresh parsley.

SAUTÉED BRUSSELS SPROUTS WITH GARLIC

Bright green Brussels sprouts complement the mushrooms and pepper beautifully for an eye-appealing and tasty dish.

2 tbs. *Garlic Herb Butter*, page 29
1 lb. fresh Brussels sprouts
2 tbs. vegetable or canola oil
3 cloves garlic, minced or squeezed through a press
1 cup thinly sliced mushrooms
1 red bell pepper, cut into matchstick strips
1/4 cup roasted pecans or cashews, optional

Prepare *Garlic Herb Butter* and set aside. Remove outer leaves and cut Brussels sprouts into quarters. Heat oil in a large skillet. Add garlic and sauté for 1 minute. Add Brussels sprouts, mushrooms and pepper. Sauté for 5 to 7 minutes. Transfer to a serving bowl and toss with *Garlic Herb Butter*. For added flavor and crunch, sprinkle with roasted pecans or cashews after cooking.

STRING BEAN AND GARLIC MIX

This deeply flavorful vegetable dish tastes great hot or cold. It's a good addition to a picnic, and it's easy to prepare, too.

1 lb. string beans
3 tbs. olive oil
¾ tsp. garlic powder
¼ tsp. dried basil
freshly ground pepper to taste

Snip tips off both ends of beans with kitchen shears or cut off with a sharp knife. Break beans in half. Wash beans under cold running water. Place beans in a 2½- to 3½-quart saucepan with 1 inch water and steam or boil until tender, about 4 minutes. Remove beans, without liquid, from saucepan. If you are serving them cold, plunge beans into cold water for 1 to 2 minutes, drain and place in a storage container or bowl. If you are serving them hot, remove to a serving bowl. Add olive oil, garlic powder, basil and pepper. Mix thoroughly. Serve hot or refrigerate and serve cold.

FRESH BROCCOLI WITH SLICED GARLIC

Servings: 4

This is a wonderful accompaniment to poultry and fish dishes. Serve with lots of crusty bread for dipping. Use broccoli rabe (also called rape, rapini or broccoli raab) instead of broccoli for a unique variation.

4 cups broccoli, or broccoli rabe, florets and sliced stems
4 cloves garlic, cut into ¼-inch slices
¼ cup olive oil
¼ tsp. dried basil
¼ tsp. freshly ground pepper

Pour ½ inch water into a 2½- to 3½-quart saucepan. Add broccoli, garlic slices, olive oil and spices. Mix thoroughly. Bring water to a boil. Cover and cook over low heat for 5 minutes. Serve immediately as a side dish in individual deep bowls with garlic-flavored liquid. The liquid keeps the broccoli hot and adds flavor.

SAUTÉED ZUCCHINI BLOSSOMS

Watch out for the bees if you pick the blossoms from your own vegetable garden. Be sure to wait until late morning when the flowers are completely open. Bees are often trapped inside the closed flowers from the night before. Blossoms from other summer squash substitute very nicely.

12 zucchini blossoms
4 tbs. *Garlic Herb Butter*, page 29
½ cup flour
½ tsp. garlic powder
2 tsp. freshly grated Parmesan cheese
2 eggs, beaten

Cut off the long stem and tiny tough outer leaves of each zucchini blossom and set aside. Prepare *Garlic Herb Butter*. In a medium bowl, combine flour, garlic powder and Parmesan cheese. Heat 1 tbs. *Garlic Herb Butter* in a nonstick skillet. Add more butter as needed. Dip blossoms into eggs and coat with flour mixture. Sauté each side of blossom for about 3 minutes, or until golden brown. Serve warm.

GARLICKY VEGETABLE SAUTÉ

This spicy and satisfying vegetable recipe can easily be increased if you need more servings.

2 tbs. olive or vegetable oil
$\frac{1}{2}$ tsp. paprika
$\frac{1}{2}$ cup sliced scallions
4 cloves garlic, minced or squeezed through a press
1 medium red bell pepper, cut into thin matchstick strips
1 medium green bell pepper, cut into thin matchstick strips
1 medium yellow summer squash, sliced into $\frac{1}{8}$-inch rounds
1 medium zucchini, sliced into $\frac{1}{8}$-inch rounds
$\frac{1}{4}$ tsp. freshly ground pepper

Heat oil in a large skillet over medium heat. Add paprika and stir thoroughly. Add scallions and garlic; sauté for 2 minutes. Add all other ingredients, partially cover and sauté over medium-low heat for 15 to 17 minutes, or until vegetables are tender, stirring occasionally.

GUACAMOLE

*Serve with **Garlic Pita Chips**, page 26, raw vegetables or as a salad topping. For a variation, mix in diced tomatoes, sliced olives or chopped hard-cooked eggs and serve as a sandwich spread.*

2 ripe avocados
1 can (4.5 oz.) green chili peppers, finely chopped
4 cloves garlic, minced or squeezed through a press
juice of 1 lime
1 medium onion, finely chopped
3 tbs. finely chopped fresh cilantro
1 tbs. finely chopped jalapeño peppers
1 tsp. chili powder
1/8 tsp. ground cumin
1/8 tsp. freshly ground pepper
1/8 tsp. salt

Peel avocados and remove pits; mash in a bowl with a fork until smooth but a little chunky. Combine with remaining ingredients, cover and refrigerate for 2 hours.

BROCCOLI AND GARLIC STIR-FRY

Servings: 4

Serve as a side dish with meats, poultry or seafood. It's also exceptionally flavorful as an entrée over white rice on individual serving plates.

1 lb. fresh broccoli florets and stems
2 tsp. sesame seeds
1 tbs. safflower, sunflower or peanut oil
6 cloves garlic, minced or squeezed through a press
$\frac{1}{2}$ tsp. grated ginger root
1 tbs. low sodium soy sauce
$\frac{1}{4}$ cup water

Chop broccoli florets into 1-inch pieces and cut stems into matchstick strips. Roast sesame seeds in a dry skillet over medium heat, stirring constantly, until seeds are golden brown. Heat oil over medium-high heat in a skillet or wok. Add garlic and ginger root and sauté for 1 minute. Add broccoli, soy sauce and water. Stir-fry for 4 minutes. Transfer broccoli to a serving bowl and mix in sesame seeds.

MASHED POTATOES
WITH ROASTED GARLIC

I prefer to mash the potatoes with an old-fashioned hand masher because I like my potatoes slightly lumpy. If you're not a fan of lumpy potatoes, process the ingredients with an electric mixer until lump-free and fluffy. You'll find a high-quality potato peeler an indispensable tool in your kitchen.

1 medium bulb garlic, roasted (see
  page 64)
2 lb. (about 6) potatoes
1/2 cup milk

1/4 cup butter
1/4 tsp. freshly ground pepper
chopped fresh parsley, optional

Prepare roasted garlic. Peel potatoes and cut into quarters. Place potatoes in a deep pot of cold water. Water should just cover potatoes. Cover pot and bring to a boil. Reduce heat and simmer for 20 minutes, or until tender. Carefully drain potatoes. Heat potatoes in pot over low heat to dry, stirring or shaking continuously. Mash potatoes with a strong masher. Slowly add milk and mash continuously. Squeeze roasted garlic from each clove and add to potatoes with butter and pepper. Mash thoroughly. Transfer to serving plates or a warm ceramic bowl. For best flavor, eat immediately. Garnish with chopped parsley.

GARLIC AND HONEY CARROTS

Servings: 4

Choose young, tender carrots for a sweet, full flavor. You'll cook this dish again!

3 cups carrots, sliced into ¼-inch rounds
2 tbs. butter
1 tbs. honey
1 clove garlic, minced or squeezed through a press
1 tsp. minced onion
2 tbs. raisins
1 tsp. brown sugar, firmly packed
¼ tsp. dried dill weed

Place carrots in a vegetable steamer with 1 inch water. Bring to a boil and steam for 5 to 7 minutes, or until carrots are tender-crisp.

To make sauce: While carrots are cooking, combine, butter, honey, garlic, onion, raisins, brown sugar and dill weed in a small saucepan. Cook over low heat until onion and garlic are soft.

Combine carrots and sauce in a serving bowl. Mix thoroughly. Serve warm.

PASTA

ROASTED VEGETABLES OVER LINGUINE

Servings: 4

Roasting allows the vegetables to maintain their distinctive flavors. This beautiful dish goes great with a fresh garden salad and lots of fresh Italian bread.

1 bulb garlic, roasted (see page 64)
1 medium eggplant
1 large red bell pepper
1 large green bell pepper
1 large red onion
2 medium zucchini
2 medium summer squash
1/4 cup olive oil
1/4 cup balsamic vinegar
1 cup water
1 chicken bouillon cube
16 oz. dried linguine
2 tbs. chopped fresh basil
1/2 cup freshly grated Parmesan cheese

Prepare roasted garlic. Peel eggplant and cut into ½-inch cubes. Remove stems, membranes and all seeds from peppers and cut lengthwise into ¼-inch-wide slices. Cut onion into quarters and separate layers. Slice zucchini and summer squash into ¼-inch rounds. Pierce roasted garlic with a fork to easily remove cooked cloves from skin. In a large bowl, combine garlic, eggplant, pepper, onion, zucchini and squash with olive oil and vinegar. Mix thoroughly. Arrange vegetables in a metal roasting or baking pan. Bake in a preheated 425° oven for 30 minutes. Stir occasionally. Place vegetables under the broiler for 3 minutes. Heat 1 cup water over low heat and dissolve bouillon cube. Cook linguine in a large pot according to package instructions. Drain pasta and return to pot. Add chicken bouillon, stir and keep warm over low heat. Arrange linguine on 4 warm serving plates. Divide roasted vegetables over pasta. Sprinkle with fresh basil and Parmesan cheese and serve immediately.

GARLIC AND BASIL CREAM SAUCE OVER SPAGHETTI

The Ancient Greeks referred to basil as the "royal herb." This delicious sauce transforms the pasta into a gourmet's delight.

6 oz. dried spaghetti
4 tbs. butter
4 cloves garlic, minced or squeezed through a press
1 cup light cream
1 tbs. plus 1 tsp. minced fresh basil
1/8 tsp. dried thyme
1/8 tsp. freshly ground pepper
freshly grated Parmesan cheese

Cook spaghetti in a medium pot according to package instructions. Melt butter in a small deep skillet. Add garlic and sauté for 3 minutes over low heat. Pour in cream and add 1 tbs. basil, thyme and pepper. Stir thoroughly. Simmer over medium-low heat, covered but vented, for 7 to 9 minutes, or until thickened. Stir occasionally. If sauce becomes too thick, add more cream to thin. Pour sauce over spaghetti and sprinkle with fresh basil. Serve immediately with Parmesan cheese.

PASTA WITH BASIL, GARLIC AND TOMATOES

If you're cooking with canned chicken broth, use a gravy separator to eliminate the excess fat. You can also pour it into a bowl or other container and refrigerate it until the fat solidifies, and then lift it from the broth. For added flavor, substitute dried basil with 3 tbs. chopped fresh basil.

12 oz. dried angel hair pasta
2 tbs. olive oil
8 cloves garlic, thinly sliced
2 cups chicken broth

4 cups chopped plum tomatoes
1 tbs. dried basil
freshly grated Parmesan or Romano
  cheese

Cook angel hair pasta in a large pot of boiling water for 2 to 3 minutes. Do not overcook. Drain well and set aside. Heat olive oil in a deep 3- to 4-quart skillet over medium heat. Add garlic slices and reduce heat to low. Sauté garlic until tender, about 3 to 5 minutes, but do not brown. Add chicken broth and tomato pieces, increase heat and bring to a boil. Reduce heat to low. Cover skillet and simmer for 7 minutes. Stir in basil and cook for 1 more minute. Distribute cooked pasta on 4 warm serving plates. Carefully spoon tomato-garlic mixture over pasta. Coat all the pasta with seasoned liquid. Sprinkle with Parmesan or Romano cheese.

BOW TIE PASTA WITH ROASTED GARLIC AND EGGPLANT

The fontina cheese melts from the heat of the cooked vegetables and pasta for a truly wonderful dish with an interesting roasted flavor.

1 bulb garlic, roasted (see page 64)
6 cups eggplant, peeled and cut
   into 1-inch cubes
½ cup balsamic vinegar
4 tbs. olive oil
¼ tsp. dried oregano
½ tsp. freshly ground pepper
3 cups (about 3 medium) chopped tomatoes
1 pkg. (8 oz.) dried large bow tie pasta
½ cup shredded fontina cheese
2 tbs. chopped fresh parsley
¼ cup freshly grated Parmesan cheese

Separate roasted garlic cloves, peel and set aside. In a medium bowl, combine eggplant, vinegar, 3 tbs. olive oil, oregano and pepper. Mix thoroughly and marinate in the refrigerator for 1 hour. Place eggplant mixture, with liquid, on a baking pan. Bake in a preheated 425° oven for 25 minutes. Stir every 5 to 6 minutes. About 10 minutes before eggplant is completely cooked, heat 1 tbs. olive oil in a skillet. Add tomatoes and garlic. Sauté for 5 minutes. At the same time, cook pasta in a pot of boiling water according to package instructions. Drain and divide cooked pasta on 4 serving plates. Cover pasta with roasted eggplant. Sprinkle with fontina cheese. Cover cheese with equal portions of tomato-garlic mixture and top with parsley. Serve immediately sprinkled with Parmesan cheese.

PASTA WITH PESTO

There is no comparison to fresh basil. Growing your own basil is fun, easy and economical. The plants thrive inside or outside and the pesto mixture freezes very well. Just omit the cheese before freezing and add it later.

2 cups fresh basil leaves
3 cloves garlic
1 cup olive oil
½ cup pine nuts, or chopped walnuts

¼ tsp. freshly ground pepper
½ cup grated Parmesan cheese
¼ cup pine nuts
16 oz. dried spaghetti

To prepare the pesto, combine basil, garlic, olive oil, ¼ cup nuts and pepper in a food processor or blender. Process for 15 to 20 seconds until paste forms. Pour into a bowl and mix in cheese. Roast ¼ cup pine nuts in a dry skillet over medium heat, stirring constantly until nuts are golden brown, about 2 minutes. Cook pasta in a large pot of boiling water, according to package instructions. Drain well. Toss each serving of hot pasta with ¾ cup pesto sauce. Top with roasted pine nuts and serve.

VARIATION

Fresh pasta tossed with pesto also tastes wonderful topped with a spoonful of salsa.

SHRIMP AND GARLIC FETTUCCINE ALFREDO

Fettuccine Alfredo was created in the 1920s by Italian restaurateur Alfredo di Lello. This variation is rich and remarkably flavorful.

8 tbs. butter
6 cloves garlic, minced or squeezed
    through a press
1 lb. large shrimp, peeled and deveined
3/4 cup fresh or frozen peas
12 oz. dried fettuccine

8 oz. heavy cream
3/4 cup grated Parmesan cheese
1/2 tsp. freshly ground pepper
1/4 cup finely chopped black olives
1 tbs. chopped fresh basil

Melt 2 tbs. butter in a skillet over medium heat. Add garlic and sauté for 1 minute. Add shrimp and sauté on each side for 2 to 3 minutes, or until pink. Set aside. Steam or boil peas for 3 minutes, drain and set aside. While you prepare sauce, cook fettuccine according to package instructions, drain and set aside.

To prepare sauce: Melt remaining butter in a skillet over medium heat. Reduce heat to low and whisk in cream, Parmesan cheese and pepper. Add shrimp, peas, black olives and basil. Stir well and mix with fettuccine. Serve immediately.

PASTA WITH TOMATO AND GARLIC SAUCE

The garlic provides a stimulating flavor to this classic pasta entreé.

2 tbs. olive oil
12 cloves garlic, minced or squeezed
   through a press
1 cup minced onion
1 can (28 oz.) can tomato puree
3 tbs. minced fresh basil
1 tsp. minced fresh parsley

1/4 freshly ground pepper
1/8 tsp. sugar
1 large bay leaf
12 oz. dried fettuccine or linguine
freshly grated Parmesan or Romano
   cheese

Heat olive oil in a saucepan or deep skillet. Add garlic and onion; sauté over medium heat for 7 to 10 minutes, or until soft. Add tomato puree and stir in remaining ingredients, except cheese. Simmer with cover vented over medium-low heat for 1½ hours. Stir occasionally. Cook pasta in a large pot, according to package instructions. Remove bay leaf from sauce. Pour sauce over pasta and serve sprinkled with Parmesan or Romano cheese.

PASTA WITH BROCCOLI

This is one of my personal favorites — quick, easy and very tasty. Pasta is always good with fresh Italian bread and a large garden salad.

1 lb. dried macaroni
6 cloves garlic, minced or squeezed through a press
½ cup olive oil
4 cups broccoli florets and sliced stems
½ cup freshly grated Parmesan cheese

While you make the sauce, cook macaroni in a large 5- to 6-quart pot of boiling water, according to package instructions. Do not overcook. Drain well. Combine garlic and olive oil in a small saucepan and sauté over low heat for 8 minutes. Steam broccoli in a 2- to 3-quart covered saucepan for 5 minutes. Combine cooked pasta, steamed broccoli and garlic-oil mixture in pot. Mix well and cook over low heat for 5 more minutes. Stir occasionally. Serve hot with Parmesan cheese.

PASTA AND GARLIC CHEESE SAUCE

For variety, substitute another vegetable for broccoli, or eliminate it and increase the quantity of pasta. Serve as a main course or side dish.

4 cups broccoli florets and sliced stems
16 oz. dried rigatoni, or small shells
1 tbs. olive oil
2 tbs. butter
3 tbs. flour
1 cup milk
1 tbs. fresh garlic, minced or squeezed
  through a press

1 tbs. minced onion
2 tsp. dried basil
1 tsp. dried thyme
1/2 tsp. freshly ground pepper
1 cup shredded fontina cheese
1 cup shredded mozzarella cheese
freshly grated Parmesan cheese, optional

Cook broccoli in a vegetable steamer, or boil for 5 to 6 minutes, and set aside. Cook pasta in a large pot according to package instructions. Drain pasta and return to pot. Toss pasta with olive oil and cooked broccoli. In a medium saucepan, melt butter over medium heat. Stir continuously, slowly adding flour and milk. Add garlic, onion, basil, thyme and pepper. Mix well. Add fontina and mozzarella cheeses, mixing continuously over low heat as sauce forms, about 1 to 2 minutes. Pour sauce over pasta and broccoli. Serve immediately topped with Parmesan cheese.

PASTA WITH ROASTED GARLIC
AND GREEN PEPPERS

For a colorful appearance, prepare this dish with spinach fettuccine. Substitute the sauce with your own recipe or a favorite commercially prepared brand. Serve with fresh Italian or French bread.

2 bulbs garlic, roasted (see page 64)
4 cups *Marinara Sauce*, page 71
2 tbs. olive oil
1 large green or red bell pepper, diced
1 onion, minced

1 tsp. dried basil
1/2 tsp. dried oregano
1/4 tsp. freshly ground pepper
12 oz. dried fettuccine
freshly grated Parmesan cheese

Squeeze soft garlic from each roasted garlic clove and set aside. Prepare *Marinara Sauce*. Heat olive oil in a skillet and sauté bell pepper for 3 minutes. Add onion and continue to sauté for 5 more minutes. Add pepper, onion, garlic and spices to *Marinara Sauce* and simmer for 30 minutes. Stir occasionally. Cook pasta in a large pot of boiling water, according to package instructions. Drain well. Distribute cooked pasta on warm serving plates. Top with a layer of sauce. Pass Parmesan cheese.

FETTUCCINE WITH GARLIC OIL

Serve as a main course or side dish with veal, poultry or seafood. For the best flavor, purchase Parmesan or Romano cheese in a large piece and grate it easily at home in a food processor or with a stainless steel hand-crank-style grater.

⅔ cup olive oil
10 cloves garlic
12 oz. dried fettuccine
⅓ cup chopped fresh parsley
freshly grated Parmesan or Romano cheese

In a small saucepan, heat olive oil over medium heat. Add whole garlic cloves, reduce heat to low, cover and simmer for 25 minutes. Strain garlic and save oil. Set garlic aside to cool. Cook pasta in a large pot, according to package instructions. While pasta is cooking, squeeze pulp from garlic cloves and mash. Drain pasta and return to pot. Toss pasta with oil, garlic and parsley. Top with Parmesan or Romano cheese.

PASTA WITH ROASTED GARLIC AND BASIL SAUCE

Serve as a main course or side dish with a salad and garlic bread. The highly aromatic sauce is also delicious over freshly cooked vegetables.

10 cloves garlic
4 tbs. plus ¼ tsp. safflower, sunflower or vegetable oil
1 tbs. balsamic vinegar
1 cup chopped fresh basil
¼ cup chopped fresh parsley

4 tbs. chopped walnuts, or pine nuts
3 tbs. chicken broth
½ tsp. freshly ground pepper
2 tbs. freshly grated Parmesan cheese
12 oz. dried linguine

Place garlic cloves in a garlic baker or on a nonstick or lightly oiled baking sheet; cover. Bake in a preheated 350° oven for 30 to 35 minutes. Peel skin from garlic cloves, or squeeze out garlic pulp. Combine garlic, 4 tbs. oil, vinegar, basil, parsley, nuts, chicken broth and pepper in a food processor or blender and process until smooth. Transfer to a bowl and stir in cheese; set aside or refrigerate. Cook pasta according to package instructions. Rinse pasta and drain. Remove pasta to a saucepan over low heat. Toss with garlic-basil mixture and serve.

FISH AND SHELLFISH

SWORDFISH WITH GARLIC AND FENNEL

This is a magnificent dish even for the most selective seafood lover. Garlic, fennel and lemon blend together very nicely for an interesting flavor. Use a mortar and pestle to grind the fennel.

2 lb. swordfish
6 tbs. olive oil
8 cloves garlic, thinly sliced
8 tbs. fresh lemon juice
1/2 tsp. ground fennel seeds
fresh cilantro or basil sprigs for garnish

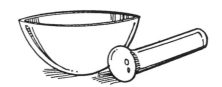

Rinse fish under cold running water and pat dry. Divide fish into 4 equal pieces. Heat 2 tbs. olive oil in a 10- or 12-inch nonstick skillet. Cook over medium heat, 2 pieces at a time, for 4 to 5 minutes on each side. Do not overcook fish. While fish is cooking, heat 4 tbs. olive oil in a small skillet. Add garlic, lemon juice and fennel. Sauté over medium heat for 5 minutes. Place cooked fish on warm individual serving plates. Cover fish with equal portions of garlic-lemon sauce. Garnish with cilantro or basil sprigs.

LOBSTER AND GARLIC SAUTÉ

This unusual and substantial dish is brimming with irresistible flavors. The recipe is a inspiration from a vacation trip spent on the seacoast in Ogunquit, Maine. Jars of fermented black beans can be found in the Oriental section of most supermarkets and in specialty food shops.

2 tbs. fermented black beans
¼ cup dry sherry
2 tsp. cornstarch
8 oz. dried fettuccine
3 tbs. peanut or vegetable oil
4 cloves garlic, squeezed through a press
1 tsp. grated ginger root
¼ cup chicken stock
¼ cup chopped scallions
2 cups chopped broccoli florets and sliced stems
⅓ cup thinly sliced water chestnuts
½ lb. fresh cooked lobster meat, cut into bite-sized pieces
½ cup water

In a small bowl, combine fermented black beans, sherry and cornstarch. Mix thoroughly to form a sauce and set aside. In a large pot of boiling water, cook fettuccine according to package instructions. Drain well and set aside. Heat 2 tbs. oil in a small saucepan. Add 1 pressed garlic clove and ½ tsp. ginger root. Cook for 2 minutes. Add chicken stock and bring to a quick boil. Toss with pasta. Keep warm in a large pot on very low heat. Heat remaining oil in a large skillet or wok over medium heat. Add remaining garlic, ginger root and scallions. Sauté for 2 minutes. Add broccoli and water chestnuts. Stir and cook for 3 minutes. Add lobster, water and bean sauce. Stir frequently and cook uncovered for 2 to 3 minutes, or until lobster is just warm. Serve over fettuccine on individual serving plates.

SAUTÉED SHRIMP WITH GARLIC AND ONION

Servings: 4

A shrimp cleaner is inexpensive, easy to use and will greatly reduce the time spent preparing this and other shrimp recipes. Serve this dish with pasta and salad.

2 lb. fresh or frozen large shrimp
1 tsp. paprika
½ tsp. dried thyme
½ tsp. dried chervil
¼ tsp. dried marjoram
¼ tsp. ground sea salt
1 tsp. freshly ground pepper

1 tsp. plus 2 tbs. butter
6 cloves garlic, minced or squeezed
   through a press
1 medium onion, minced
1 tbs. fresh lemon juice
1 lemon, cut into wedges
1 tbs. minced fresh basil

Peel and devein shrimp. Wash under cold running water. Drain and dry with paper towels. In a small bowl, combine paprika, thyme, chervil, marjoram, salt and pepper. Toss shrimp with herbs and set aside. Heat 1 tsp. butter in a large skillet over medium heat and sauté garlic and onion until lightly browned, about 3 minutes. Remove from skillet and set aside. Heat 2 tbs. butter in skillet and sauté shrimp for 2 minutes. Add garlic, onion and lemon juice and sauté for 1 minute. Transfer to individual serving plates, each with a few lemon wedges. Sprinkle with fresh basil and serve.

BAKED MACKEREL

You should only cook fresh fish. Always insist on smelling the fish and don't purchase fish that has a strong fishy odor. Fresh mackerel should have shiny skin, firm and moist flesh and a mild ocean odor.

2 tbs. olive or vegetable oil
8 cloves garlic, minced or squeezed
  through a press
2 cans (14.5 oz. each) diced stewed
  tomatoes, with juice
2 medium zucchini, sliced into ¼-inch
  rounds
½ lb. mushrooms, thinly sliced

½ tsp. dried marjoram
½ tsp. dried oregano
½ tsp. dried basil
½ tsp. chili powder
¼ tsp. ground cumin
2 lb. mackerel fillets, or bluefish, rain-
  bow trout, lake trout or whitefish fillets

Heat oil in a small saucepan over medium-low heat. Add garlic and sauté for 4 minutes. Set aside and allow to cool. In a large bowl, combine garlic with remaining ingredients, except fish, and mix thoroughly. Rinse fish under cold running water and pat dry. Place fish in an ovenproof baking dish and cover with garlic-tomato sauce. Bake uncovered in a preheated 400° oven for 30 minutes.

BAKED STUFFED SHRIMP

Roasted garlic and shrimp combine perfectly for a spectacular meal.

1 bulb garlic, roasted (see page 64)
3 tbs. butter
1/4 cup finely chopped green bell
  pepper
1 small onion, finely chopped
1/2 cup breadcrumbs

1/4 tsp. dried thyme
1/4 tsp. freshly ground pepper
1/4 tsp. salt
2 tbs. freshly grated Parmesan cheese
8 jumbo shrimp, shelled and deveined
3 tbs. butter, melted

Separate roasted garlic cloves, peel and mash in a small bowl to form a paste. Melt butter in a skillet over medium heat. Add green pepper and onion; sauté for 4 minutes. Add garlic paste and sauté for 3 minutes. Add breadcrumbs, thyme, pepper and salt; sauté for 3 minutes. Add Parmesan cheese. Mix well and allow to cool. Butterfly shrimp and place in an ovenproof baking dish. Roll stuffing into eight 1 1/4-inch balls. Place a ball of stuffing on top of each shrimp. Drizzle with melted butter. Bake in a preheated 400° oven for 7 to 10 minutes, or until shrimp are pink. Serve immediately.

SPICY TUNA STEAKS

A nonstick grilling rack designed for cooking on an outdoor barbecue is the perfect solution for keeping fish and other delicate foods from sticking, burning and falling apart. These are delicious served with roasted vegetables.

¼ cup vegetable or olive oil
6 cloves garlic, minced or
  squeezed through a press
3 tbs. low sodium soy sauce
¼ tsp. dry mustard
3 tbs. fresh lemon juice
½ tsp. freshly ground pepper
2 lb. tuna steaks
1 lemon, cut into wedges

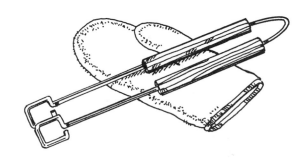

In a medium bowl, combine oil, garlic, soy sauce, mustard, lemon juice and pepper. Mix well. Rinse fish under cold running water and pat dry. Place fish in a shallow bowl and cover with marinade. Refrigerator for 1 hour. Cook fish under a preheated broiler for 5 to 7 minutes on each side, or until opaque, or grill fish on an outdoor barbecue. Serve with lemon wedges.

BAKED SALMON WITH SLICED GARLIC

My dad, an avid salt water fisherman and fabulous cook, once told me that the secret to great-tasting salmon is simple. Just be sure it's fresh and cook it with lots of garlic. Add a garden salad and fresh rolls. Absolutely perfect!

2 lb. salmon
1/3 cup olive oil
4 cloves garlic, cut into 1/4-inch slices
1/4 tsp. dried basil
1/4 tsp. dried parsley
1/4 tsp. freshly ground pepper

Rinse fish under cold running water and pat dry. Cut fish into 4 equal pieces, and place in a shallow stainless steel or ceramic baking dish. Liberally coat all sides of fish with some of the olive oil. Do not allow fish pieces to overlap. Pour remaining olive oil over fish. Cover top layers of fish with garlic slices. Sprinkle with basil, parsley and pepper. Bake uncovered in a preheated 375° oven for 20 minutes.

BROILED HADDOCK WITH GARLIC AND BASIL

Almost any delicate white fish such as catfish or flounder will substitute nicely.

2 lb. haddock or cod fillets
4 tbs. olive oil
1/4 cup seasoned breadcrumbs
1/4 tsp. freshly ground pepper
1/4 tsp. paprika
2 cloves garlic, minced or
   squeezed through a press
1/2 tsp. dried basil
1 lemon, cut into wedges

Rinse fish under cold running water and pat dry. Place fish in a metal ovenproof baking pan and coat all sides with 2 tbs. olive oil. Cover top of fish with a thin layer of breadcrumbs. Season with pepper and sprinkle with paprika. Broil fish under a preheated broiler for 8 to 10 minutes, or until fish is opaque. While fish is cooking, heat 2 tbs. olive oil in a small saucepan. Add garlic and basil. Sauté for 2 minutes over medium heat. Pour garlic-basil mixture over fish on individual serving plates. Serve with lemon wedges.

BAKED COD

You may replace the cod with halibut, red snapper, flounder or haddock. Find a good fish market where you're sure the fish is always fresh and properly cleaned.

2 tbs. *Garlic Herb Butter*, page 29
4 (8 oz. each) cod steaks
2 tsp. dried lemon peel
1 cup breadcrumbs
1 cup skim milk
1/4 tsp. vegetable or olive oil

2 tbs. fresh lemon juice
1 tsp. minced fresh tarragon, or 1/2 tsp. dried
2 cloves garlic, minced or squeezed through a press

Prepare *Garlic Herb Butter*, and set aside. Rinse fish under cold running water and pat dry. In a shallow bowl, mix together lemon peel and breadcrumbs. Pour milk in another shallow bowl and coat all sides of fish with milk. Dredge fish with breadcrumbs and place in a lightly oiled ovenproof baking dish. Drizzle with lemon juice and sprinkle with tarragon and garlic. Dot with *Garlic Herb Butter*. Bake in a preheated 400° oven for 8 to 10 minutes, or until fish is just opaque.

SKEWERED TUNA WITH GARLIC MARINADE

Cubes of tuna are infused with a garlic marinade and accompanied by fresh vegetables. You'll find this satisfying and enormously flavorful. Serve with a garden salad.

12 oz. *Basic Garlic Salad Dressing and Marinade*, page 55
2 medium onions
2 medium green bell peppers

1 lb. tuna
16 fresh mushrooms, whole
16 cherry tomatoes
lemon wedges

Prepare marinade, tripling all ingredients. Cut onions into quarters and separate layers. Cut peppers into 1-inch pieces. Rinse fish under cold running water and pat dry. Cut fish into 1-inch cubes, and place in a shallow bowl with onions, peppers, mushrooms and tomatoes. Pour marinade over fish and vegetables. Cover bowl and refrigerate for 3 hours, or overnight. Alternately thread fish, onions, peppers, mushrooms and tomatoes onto 6 to 8 stainless steel or presoaked bamboo skewers. Place on a hot grill or under a preheated broiler for 8 minutes. Baste with marinade and turn once. Serve with lemon wedges.

GARLICKY SWORDFISH

This grilled swordfish has a pleasing flavor without even a hint of mayonnaise taste.

2 (8 oz. each) swordfish steaks
¼ cup *Garlic Mayonnaise*, page 56
1 tsp. dried dill weed

Combine *Garlic Mayonnaise* with dill weed. Mix well. Rinse fish under cold running water and pat dry. Spread a layer of mayonnaise on both sides of fish. Place swordfish steaks on a rack over a medium-hot grill. Cook for 5 to 6 minutes on each side, or until thickest section is opaque when you cut into it with a knife.

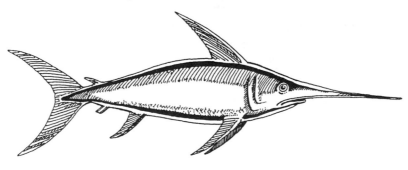

SHRIMP SCAMPI

Absolutely delightful! This dish has 70 percent less fat than most scampi recipes and is just as flavorful.

1 medium bulb garlic, roasted for 45 minutes (see page 64)
1 lb. fresh or frozen large shrimp
2 tbs. butter
4 cloves garlic, minced or squeezed through a press
2 tbs. olive oil

⅓ cup dry sherry
2 tbs. fresh lemon juice
1 tbs. chopped fresh parsley
¼ tsp. salt, optional
6 oz. spinach fettuccine, cooked according to package instructions, optional

Separate roasted garlic cloves, peel and set aside. Peel and devein shrimp. Wash under cold running water and pat dry. Melt butter in a small saucepan. Add minced or squeezed garlic, olive oil, sherry, lemon juice, parsley and salt. Place shrimp in a shallow ovenproof baking dish. Do not allow shrimp to overlap. Arrange roasted garlic cloves among shrimp. Pour sauce over shrimp and garlic cloves. Bake in a preheated 450° oven for 5 minutes. Place under a preheated broiler for 5 minutes. Serve immediately on warm individual serving plates or over hot spinach fettuccine.

HALIBUT WITH GARLICKY SUN-DRIED TOMATO PESTO

Refrigerate the extra pesto and use as a dipping sauce for calzones, or toss with fresh pasta.

2 cloves garlic
¼ cup chopped sun-dried tomatoes, reconstituted
¼ cup chopped fresh tomatoes
1 cup fresh basil leaves
½ cup olive oil
¼ cup pine nuts, or chopped walnuts

⅛ tsp. freshly ground pepper
¼ cup freshly grated Parmesan cheese
4 (8 oz. each) halibut steaks, 1 inch thick
½ tsp. butter, room temperature
fresh parsley or cilantro sprigs for garnish

To make pesto, combine garlic, sun-dried tomatoes, fresh tomatoes, basil, olive oil, nuts and pepper in a blender or food processor. Puree for 15 to 20 seconds, until a paste forms. Pour into a bowl and mix in Parmesan cheese. Set aside. Rinse fish under cold running water and pat dry; place in 1 large or 4 individual lightly buttered dishes. Spread a layer of pesto over each piece of fish. Cover with aluminum foil or parchment paper. Bake in a preheated 475° oven for 20 minutes. Garnish with fresh parsley or cilantro sprigs.

PAN-FRIED SWORDFISH WITH GARLIC SALSA Servings: 2

Simple to prepare, spicy and satisfying. The salsa gives this dish a vibrant presentation. For an alternative, substitute fresh sea bass, tuna or bluefish.

½ cup *Garlic Salsa*, page 25
2 (8 oz. each) swordfish steaks
1 tbs. olive oil
¼ tsp. freshly ground pepper
fresh parsley sprigs for garnish

Prepare *Garlic Salsa*. Rinse fish under cold running water and pat dry. Heat olive oil over medium heat in a nonstick skillet and add pepper. Place fish in skillet and cook for 4 minutes. Turn fish over and spread a layer of *Garlic Salsa* on cooked side. Cover skillet and cook on medium-low heat for 4 more minutes. Transfer fish to serving plates. Serve with remaining salsa on the side for dipping. Garnish with parsley sprigs.

PARCHMENT SALMON
WITH ROASTED GARLIC

Parchment paper is absolutely wonderful for cooking seafood. This is an exciting and delicious recipe to prepare and serve. Serve with a crisp green salad and some crusty bread.

1 bulb garlic, roasted (see page 64)
4 (6-8 oz. each) salmon steaks
4 oz. cream cheese
1 medium firm tomato, chopped
3 tbs. chopped fresh basil
½ tsp. ground dill weed
½ tsp. freshly ground pepper
1 tbs. olive oil
2 tbs. freshly grated Parmesan cheese
2 tbs. fresh lemon juice
8 lemon wedges

Squeeze pulp from roasted garlic cloves and set aside. Rinse fish under cold running water and pat dry. In a medium bowl, combine garlic, cream cheese, tomato, basil, dill and pepper. Mix thoroughly until a paste forms. Lay out four 15-x-18-inch sheets of parchment paper. Brush entire surface of one side of each sheet with olive oil. Fold parchment paper sheets in half so oiled sides are facing each other. Unfold and sprinkle one side of each sheet with Parmesan cheese. Place 1 salmon steak on top of cheese next to fold. Spread equal portions of garlic-cream cheese mixture on each piece of salmon. Drizzle with lemon juice. Fold and tightly seal each packet by overlapping small 1/4-inch folds along 3 sides, or a series of long, thin folds. Place packets on baking sheets and bake in a preheated 400° oven for 20 minutes. Transfer packets to individual serving plates, allowing guests to open packets at the table. Serve with lemon wedges.

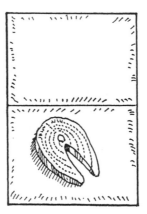
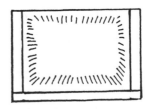

SHRIMP AND GARLIC STIR-FRY

This makes a gratifying meal full of flavor and lavish colors. Most of the preparation can be done in advance, so the cook can relax and enjoy the evening. Serve over pasta or fresh lettuce for a variation.

¼ cup almond slices
2 tbs. peanut or vegetable oil
2 tbs. butter
2 celery stalks, cut diagonally into
   ¼-inch slices
½ cup sliced scallions
6 cloves garlic, minced or squeezed
   through a press

2 cloves garlic, thinly sliced
1 red bell pepper, cut into matchstick
   strips
1 medium zucchini, cut into matchstick
   strips
½ cup dried sun-dried tomato pieces
1 lb. large shrimp, shelled and deveined
steamed white rice

Roast almond slices in a dry skillet over medium heat, stirring constantly until almonds are golden brown; set aside. Heat oil and butter in a large skillet or wok over medium heat. Add celery, scallions and all the garlic. Sauté for 3 minutes. Add pepper, zucchini and sun-dried tomatoes. Mix and cover. Simmer over low heat for 5 minutes. Add shrimp. Stir and sauté over medium-high heat until shrimp turn pink, about 2 to 3 minutes. Serve over rice. Scatter almond slices on top.

POULTRY

GARLIC LOVERS' CHICKEN

Servings: 4

Thirty cloves of garlic, slowly cooked, create a sauce with splendid aromas and a surprisingly subtle garlic flavor.

2½-3 lb. chicken pieces, legs, breasts
  or thighs
2 tbs. butter
1¼ cups chicken broth
½ cup white wine
½ cup tomato juice
2 tbs. flour

30 cloves garlic
1 bay leaf
1 tsp. dried thyme
¼ tsp. freshly ground pepper
¼ tsp. salt
cooked white rice or pasta

Rinse chicken pieces and pat dry. Heat butter in a large skillet and brown chicken pieces on each side over medium-high heat. Remove chicken from skillet and set aside. Add chicken broth, wine, tomato juice and flour to skillet. Stir and bring to a quick boil. Reduce heat to low. Add garlic, bay leaf, thyme, pepper, salt and chicken. Cover and simmer for 1 hour and 15 minutes. Remove chicken. Pour sauce through a gravy separator, or skim off fat from top of liquid. Serve chicken on individual serving plates with white rice or pasta and top with sauce.

CHICKEN AND GARLIC STIR-FRY

Servings: 2

This is a great dish with reduced fat. It's tasty, has beautiful color and is economical. As with most Chinese dishes, prepare all the ingredients before you begin to cook.

1 cup white rice
2 chicken breast halves, skinned and
  boned
2 tbs. safflower, sunflower or peanut oil
1/4 cup low sodium soy sauce
1/2 tsp. grated ginger root

4 large cloves garlic, thinly sliced
3 medium carrots, peeled and cut into
  thin matchstick strips
4 cups broccoli florets and chopped
  stems
2 tbs. water

Prepare rice in a steamer or saucepan. Rinse chicken, pat dry and cut into 1-inch cubes. Heat oil over medium-high heat in a large skillet or wok. Add chicken and sauté for 4 to 5 minutes. Reduce heat to medium. Add soy sauce, ginger, garlic, carrots, broccoli and water. Stir, cover and reduce heat to a low simmer for 5 minutes. Remove from skillet and serve over rice.

GARLIC AND OREGANO CHICKEN

*This scrumptious chicken dish is one of my favorites — an outstanding combination of ingredients. I serve it regularly and it's always a hit. Serve with **Garlic Roasted Potatoes**, page 74.*

4 chicken breast halves, skinned and
  boned
½ cup skim milk
½ cup seasoned breadcrumbs
2 tbs. olive oil
2 tbs. butter

6 cloves garlic, minced or squeezed
  through a press
2 tbs. dried oregano
¼ cup dry sherry
1 cup shredded fontina cheese
1 cup diced tomato

Rinse chicken and pat dry. Dip chicken into skim milk. Coat each side with breadcrumbs and shake off excess. Heat olive oil in a skillet and sauté each side of chicken for 10 minutes; set aside. Melt butter in a small saucepan. Add garlic, oregano and sherry. Mix and set aside. Place chicken breasts on a baking sheet, making sure pieces do not overlap. Spread a layer of cheese over each breast. Cover cheese with a layer of diced tomatoes. Slowly pour oregano mixture over tomatoes, covering each piece of chicken. Place under a preheated broiler for 2 to 3 minutes.

SKEWERED CHICKEN WITH SLICED GARLIC

Servings: 4

I use a stainless steel garlic "mandolin" (see page 12) for slicing the garlic into thin pieces. It's easy to use, reasonably priced and is available at most gourmet shops. Serve these kabobs with white rice and a garden salad.

1 cup *Garlicky Vinaigrette*, page 52
4 chicken breast halves, skinned and
  boned
1 large green bell pepper

1 large white or red onion
16 cloves garlic
1 large tomato

Prepare *Garlicky Vinaigrette*. Rinse chicken, pat dry and cut into 1-inch cubes. Combine chicken and vinaigrette in a large bowl and marinate chicken in the refrigerator for 2 hours. Cut pepper into 1-inch pieces. Cut onion into quarters and separate layers. Peel and slice garlic into thin 1/8-inch slices. Cut tomato into 8 wedges and cut each wedge in half to create 16 pieces. Alternately thread chicken cubes, garlic, pepper, garlic, onion, garlic and tomato pieces onto eight 10-inch metal or presoaked bamboo skewers. Be sure to thread slices of garlic between pieces of food. Place skewers in a preheated broiler or on a medium-high grill and cook for 10 to 12 minutes. Turn and brush with marinade occasionally.

CHICKEN PESTO

Serve as a robust lunch or dinner with fresh vegetables and garlic bread.

PESTO

2 cups fresh basil leaves
3 cloves garlic
1 cup olive oil
½ cup pine nuts, or chopped walnuts
½ tsp. freshly ground pepper
½ cup freshly grated Parmesan cheese

Combine basil, garlic, olive oil, nuts and pepper in a food processor or blender. Process for 15 to 20 seconds, or until a paste forms. Pour into a bowl and mix in Parmesan cheese. Set aside.

1 whole chicken, 4-5 lb.
1 clove garlic, thinly sliced
1 tbs. olive oil
¼ tsp. dried thyme

¼ tsp. freshly ground pepper
2 tbs. butter, melted
fresh lettuce

Remove giblets from chicken. Rinse chicken and pat dry. Tuck garlic slices under skin and rub skin with olive oil. Sprinkle chicken with thyme and pepper. Place chicken on a rack, breast side up, in a shallow ovenproof roasting pan. Bake in a preheated 325° oven for 2 to 2½ hours, or until it reaches 180° on an instant-read meat thermometer. Baste with butter and pan drippings every 15 to 20 minutes. Remove from oven and allow to cool. Discard skin and cut meat into bite-sized pieces. Toss chicken pieces with pesto. Serve warm or cold on lettuce-lined serving plates.

JOANNE'S CHICKEN AND GARLIC CHILI

Servings: 4-6

Joanne Foran has diligently worked with me on testing and developing this special collection of delicious garlic recipes. She is truly a gifted cook. This is her own version of chili. It's the best I've ever had!

1 tbs. olive oil
6 cloves garlic, minced or squeezed through a press
2 medium onions, diced
2 medium green bell peppers, diced
2 cans (14.5 oz. each) stewed tomatoes, chopped, with juice
1 can (15.5 oz.) pinto beans, drained
1 can (28 oz.) crushed tomatoes
1 tsp. ground cumin
6 tbs. chili powder
1/3 cup all-purpose flour
1 lb. chicken, cooked and sliced

In a large stockpot heat olive oil and sauté garlic, onions and green peppers over medium heat until tender. Add remaining ingredients and mix well. Bring to a boil, reduce heat to low, cover and simmer for 1½ hours.

134 POULTRY

BAKED GARLIC AND HERB CHICKEN BREAST

This is an ideal mid-week recipe for someone with a busy schedule. Just prepare the dish the night before and place the chicken in the oven when you get home, allowing yourself plenty of time to put together a crisp, fresh garden salad.

4 chicken breast halves, skinned and boned
1/4 cup olive oil
3 tbs. fresh lemon juice
4 cloves garlic, minced or squeezed through a press
2 tbs. minced onion
1 tsp. dried basil
1 tsp. dried thyme
1/2 tsp. freshly ground pepper

Rinse chicken under cold water and pat dry. Combine all ingredients, except chicken, in a bowl and mix thoroughly. Arrange chicken breasts in an ovenproof baking dish and cover with garlic-herb marinade. Refrigerate for 2 hours, or overnight. Do not overlap chicken. Bake chicken in marinade in a preheated 375° oven for 40 minutes.

PARCHMENT CHICKEN WITH ROASTED GARLIC

Parchment paper is ideal for baking chicken. It can be found in most supermarkets and specialty kitchenware shops, and through mail-order catalogs. Nothing sticks to the paper and the cleanup is quick and easy. Serve with vegetables or a salad.

1 bulb garlic, roasted (see page 64)
1/4 tsp. dried thyme
1/4 tsp. dried basil
1/4 tsp. dried parsley
1/4 tsp. dried marjoram
4 chicken breast halves, skinned and boned
1/2 cup skim milk
1/2 cup seasoned breadcrumbs
3 tbs. olive oil

Peel roasted garlic cloves, squeeze pulp from cloves and set aside. In a small bowl, combine garlic, thyme, basil, parsley and marjoram. Mix thoroughly. Rinse chicken under cold water and pat dry. Pour milk into a shallow dish and dip chicken in milk.

Coat each side of chicken with breadcrumbs and shake off excess. Heat olive oil in a skillet and sauté chicken for 2 minutes on each side. Remove chicken from skillet and set aside. Lay out four 18-x-15-inch sheets parchment paper and fold in half. Unfold parchment paper sheets and place 1 chicken breast on each parchment paper sheet next to the fold. Spread ¼ garlic mixture on top of each breast. Fold and tightly seal each packet by overlapping ¼-inch folds along sides, or a series of long, thin folds. Place packets on baking sheets in a preheated 375° oven for 30 minutes. Transfer packets to individual serving plates, allowing guests to open packets at the table.

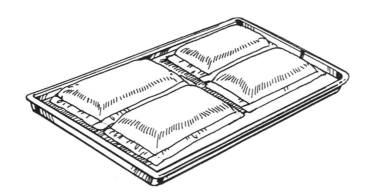

CRISPY AROMATIC CHICKEN

This savory chicken dish has an irresistible Oriental flavor.

2 chicken breast halves, skinned and boned
1 cup cornstarch
1 cup all-purpose flour
1 cup water
1 egg
1 tsp. baking powder
1 cup plus 1 tbs. canola or peanut oil
1 tbs. minced ginger root
3 cloves garlic, minced
4 cups broccoli florets and sliced stems
1 medium red or green bell pepper, cut into 1-inch pieces
1 can (8 oz.) water chestnuts, drained
Sauce, follows
steamed white rice

Rinse chicken, pat dry and cut into 1-inch cubes. Combine cornstarch, flour, water, egg and baking powder. Mix thoroughly. Heat 1 cup oil in a wok or large skillet. Dip chicken pieces in batter and sauté in oil for 10 to 12 minutes, or until golden brown on all sides. Set chicken aside and remove oil from skillet. Heat remaining 1 tbs. oil in skillet. Add ginger and garlic. Stir-fry for 1 minute. Add broccoli, bell pepper and water chestnuts. Stir-fry for 2 minutes. Add *Sauce* and chicken. Stir, cover and cook for 3 to 4 minutes. Serve hot with sauce over steamed white rice.

SAUCE

1 clove garlic, thinly sliced
1/4 cup low sodium soy sauce
1/2 cup brown sugar, firmly packed
1 medium onion, diced
1 tbs. honey

Combine ingredients in a bowl. Mix thoroughly.

CHICKEN CUTLETS

These are so delicious and such a great crowd-pleaser that a tomato or marinara sauce isn't necessary. The recipe can easily be adapted for smaller or larger quantities. These can be prepared a day in advance. Just reheat in a preheated oven at 325° for 10 to 15 minutes.

4 chicken breast halves, skinned and
  boned
1 cup seasoned breadcrumbs
½ tsp. garlic powder
2 tbs. freshly grated Parmesan cheese

½ tsp. dried basil
¼ tsp. freshly ground pepper
½ cup olive oil
1 egg, beaten

Rinse chicken under cold running water and pat dry. Fillet each breast into 3 thin cutlets. Tenderize each cutlet with a wooden or metal mallet. In a shallow bowl, combine breadcrumbs, garlic powder, cheese, basil and pepper. Heat olive oil over medium heat in a large skillet. Start with 3 tbs. olive oil and add more as needed. If cooking in an electric frying pan, set temperature at 350°. Dip cutlets in egg and coat with breadcrumb mixture. Shake off excess. Sauté each piece of chicken for 5 to 6 minutes on each side, or until golden brown. Place cooked cutlets on a paper towel-lined platter to absorb excess oil.

GARLIC CHICKEN BISTRO

This is a hearty, sumptuous recipe for boneless chicken breasts stuffed with a spicy blend of minced vegetables and topped with tomato sauce and melted cheese.

8 chicken breast halves, skinned and boned
6 cloves garlic, minced or squeezed through a press
1/3 cup minced sun-dried tomatoes, reconstituted
1/2 cup minced marinated artichoke hearts
1/4 cup minced black olives

2 tbs. minced onion
1/4 cup minced green bell pepper
1/2 tsp. dried basil
1/4 tsp. freshly ground pepper
3 cups tomato sauce
1/2 cup shredded fontina cheese
1 tbs. grated Parmesan cheese
chopped fresh parsley for garnish

Rinse chicken and pat dry. In a medium bowl, combine garlic, sun-dried tomatoes, artichoke hearts, olives, onion, green peppers, basil and pepper. Mix thoroughly. Place 4 chicken breasts in an ovenproof casserole. Spread 1/4 of mixture on top of each breast. Cover each breast with another chicken breast. Spoon the tomato sauce on top of chicken and sprinkle with fontina and Parmesan cheeses. Bake uncovered in a preheated 375° oven for 40 minutes. Garnish with parsley and serve immediately.

CHICKEN FAJITAS

An oval cast iron or anodized aluminum skillet is ideal for preparing fajitas. It heats up quickly, maintains the temperature and creates an interesting presentation at the table.

4 chicken breast halves, skinned and
  boned
3 cloves garlic, squeezed through a
  press
3 tbs. olive oil
¼ cup fresh lime juice

½ tsp. dried oregano
½ tsp. freshly ground pepper
8 corn or flour tortillas
shredded lettuce, refried beans,
  chopped onions, guacamole, salsa
  and sour cream, optional

Rinse chicken and pat dry. Slice chicken into ½-inch-wide, long strips. In a shallow bowl, combine garlic, 2 tbs. olive oil, lime juice, oregano and pepper. Mix well. Add chicken strips, cover and refrigerate for 2 hours or overnight. Turn occasionally in marinade. Heat 1 tbs. olive oil in a preheated skillet. Add chicken and cook over medium-high heat for 1 minute on each side, or until browned and cooked. Serve with warm tortillas and desired fillings.

LEMON GARLIC CHICKEN

This robust dish is for the more adventuresome.

2 chicken breast halves, skinned and
   boned
1 egg
2 tbs. milk
1/2 cup flour
1 tbs. olive oil
1 cup chicken broth

1/4 cup dry sherry
juice of 1/2 lemon
1 tbs. chopped garlic
2 tbs. chopped fresh basil
8 oz. dried bow tie pasta
1/4 tsp. freshly ground pepper, optional
2 tbs. freshly grated Parmesan cheese

Rinse chicken and pat dry. Combine egg and milk in a shallow bowl. Dip chicken in egg-milk mixture. Coat with flour and shake off excess. Heat olive oil in a skillet and sauté chicken for 5 minutes on each side. Add chicken broth, sherry, lemon juice and garlic. Bring to a boil. Cover skillet, reduce heat and simmer for 20 minutes. Add basil during last 5 minutes of cooking. While chicken is cooking, cook pasta according to package instructions. Drain pasta. Place cooked chicken on a serving plate with pasta and pour lemon-garlic sauce over all. Sprinkle with pepper and Parmesan cheese.

THE ODD COUPLE

If you're looking for something different, try serving these at your next buffet. They're delicious and make a great presentation.

GARLICKY BLUEBERRY SAUCE

4 cups blueberries, fresh or frozen, thawed
2 cloves garlic, minced or squeezed through a press
3/4 cup brown sugar, firmly packed
1/4 cup sugar
1/4 cup fresh lemon juice
1/2 tsp. lemon peel
1/2 cup balsamic vinegar

Combine all ingredients in a saucepan. Bring to a boil. Reduce heat, cover and simmer for 20 minutes. Allow to cool and serve at room temperature, or refrigerate and serve cold in individual ramekins for dipping *Sautéed Chicken*.

SAUTÉED CHICKEN

4 chicken breast halves, skinned and boned
2 tbs. olive oil
2 cloves garlic, minced or squeezed through a press
1 tsp. freshly ground pepper
2 tsp. chopped fresh basil
2 tsp. chopped fresh parsley

Rinse chicken and pat dry. Cut into 1-x-2-inch pieces. Heat olive oil in a skillet. Add garlic and sauté for 1 minute. Add chicken and pepper. Sauté for 3 to 4 minutes on each side. Add basil and parsley. Sauté for 5 more minutes, or until thoroughly cooked. Serve on individual plates, or on a large serving platter lined with fresh, leafy vegetables along with *Garlicky Blueberry Sauce*.

ULTIMATE CHICKEN WINGS

Serve these on your next buffet, or take them on a picnic. They're delicious hot or cold.

2 lb. (about 12) chicken wings
1 tbs. vegetable or olive oil
4 cloves garlic, minced or squeezed
   through a press
½ cup brown sugar, firmly packed

½ tsp. ground ginger
1 tbs. honey
¼ cup low sodium soy sauce
1 medium onion, diced

Remove excess skin from chicken wings. Rinse and pat dry. Heat olive oil in a skillet and sauté chicken wings for 12 minutes over medium heat. Add more oil if needed. Combine garlic , brown sugar, ginger, honey, soy sauce and onion in a large bowl and mix thoroughly. Marinate wings in mixture for 2 hours, or overnight, in the refrigerator. Place chicken wings in a shallow baking pan with ¾ of marinade. Bake wings in a preheated 450° oven for 35 minutes. Baste occasionally with remaining marinade. Broil for 2 minutes.

LEMON DIJON AND GARLIC CHICKEN

*A treat for mustard lovers! Serve with **Garlic Roasted Potatoes**, page 74, and a garden salad.*

2 tbs. fresh lemon juice
2 tbs. Dijon mustard
3 cloves garlic, minced or
   squeezed through a press
2 tbs. vegetable or olive oil
¼ cup low sodium soy sauce
¼ tsp. freshly ground pepper
4 chicken breast halves, skinned and boned

In a medium bowl, combine lemon juice, mustard, garlic, oil, soy sauce and pepper. Mix thoroughly. Rinse chicken and pat dry. Place chicken in an ovenproof casserole. Pour marinade over chicken, cover casserole and refrigerate for 2 hours, or overnight. Place covered casserole in a preheated 350° oven for 30 minutes. Remove cover and bake for 30 more minutes, basting occasionally.

MEATS

LEMON GARLIC VEAL

The garlic is the key to this delicious sauce. Serve with linguine.

1 large egg
½ lb. veal cutlets
¼ cup flour
⅛ tsp. freshly ground pepper
4 tbs. butter
2 tbs. olive oil
4 cloves garlic, thinly sliced
2 tbs. fresh lemon juice
1 tbs. minced fresh basil

Beat egg in a shallow bowl. Cut and pound veal into thin pieces. Dip veal in egg and dredge in flour. Season both sides of veal with pepper. Melt 2 tbs. butter in a skillet. Sauté veal over medium heat on each side for 2 to 3 minutes, or until brown. While veal is cooking, heat 2 tbs. olive oil and remaining 2 tbs. butter in a small skillet. Add garlic, lemon juice and basil. Sauté over medium heat for 4 minutes. Place cooked veal on 2 individual warm serving plates. Cover each plate of veal with half the sauce and serve.

VEAL PARMIGIANA

Thin slices of turkey or chicken breast will substitute nicely for the veal.

1 large egg
2 tbs. freshly grated Parmesan cheese
1/4 tsp. garlic powder
1 cup seasoned breadcrumbs
1 lb. veal cutlets, about 1/4-1/3-inch thick
2 tbs. olive oil
2 tbs. butter
2 cloves garlic, minced or squeezed through a press
2 cups tomato sauce
1/2 cup shredded mozzarella cheese

Beat egg in a shallow bowl. Add 1 tbs. Parmesan cheese and garlic powder to breadcrumbs and mix. Dip cutlets in egg and coat with breadcrumbs. Shake off excess. Heat olive oil and butter in a large skillet. Add minced or pressed garlic and sauté for 1 minute. Add cutlets and sauté for 2 to 3 minutes on each side, or until golden brown. Spread 3/4 cup tomato sauce in an ovenproof baking dish. Arrange cutlets in a single layer over sauce. Cover cutlets with mozzarella cheese. Spread remaining sauce over mozzarella cheese and sprinkle with remaining Parmesan cheese. Bake covered in a preheated 350° oven for 20 minutes. Remove cover and bake for 5 more minutes.

VARIATION

Place a very thin slice of proscuitto on top of each cutlet and cover with cheese and sauce.

ROAST PORK WITH GARLIC SLICES

To reduce the garlic odor from your breath, try eating 2 or 3 sprigs of flat-leaf (Italian) parsley after a meal. It doesn't totally eliminate the odor, but it helps.

1 pork loin, about 4-5 lb., boned
5 cloves garlic, cut in half
1 tbs. olive oil
1/4 tsp. dried thyme
1/4 tsp. dried rosemary

1/4 tsp. dried sage
1/4 tsp. freshly ground pepper
1 medium onion, thinly sliced
8-10 small red-skinned potatoes,
   quartered

Cut garlic cloves in half. Make 10 scattered knife cuts in roast. Insert a piece of garlic into each slit. Rub roast with olive oil and season with thyme, rosemary, sage and pepper. Place pork loin in an ovenproof roasting pan; surround with onion slices and potatoes. Bake in a preheated 350° oven for 2 hours, or until it reaches 160° on an instant-read meat thermometer. Remove meat and potatoes from roasting pan. Allow roast to sit for at least 10 minutes before carving.

BEEF AND GARLIC STIR-FRY

Quick, easy and delicious. A delightful blend of vegetables and beef creates this exciting Chinese-style dish. Serve over white rice.

2 tsp. cornstarch
3 tbs. low sodium soy sauce
1/4 cup water
1/2 tsp. sugar
1/2 tsp. freshly ground pepper
3 tbs. canola, peanut or vegetable oil

5 cloves garlic, minced or squeezed
   through a press
1 lb. flank steak, thinly sliced
2 red bell peppers, sliced into matchstick strips
2 cups thinly sliced celery

In a small bowl, combine cornstarch, soy sauce, water, sugar and pepper. Set aside. Heat 2 tbs. oil in a large skillet or wok over medium-high heat. Add garlic and sauté for 20 seconds. Add beef and sauté for 3 to 4 minutes. Remove beef and set aside. Heat remaining oil in skillet. Add bell peppers and celery. Stir-fry for 3 minutes. Pour in soy sauce mixture. Add beef and stir-fry all ingredients for 2 minutes.

SKEWERED PORK STRIPS

To prevent the bamboo skewers from burning on the grill or in the broiler, soak them in cold water for 1 hour. Serve with steamed white rice or over fresh spinach.

1 lb. pork loin
2 tbs. hot water
½ cup brown sugar, firmly packed
2 cloves garlic, minced or squeezed
  through a press

2 tbs. low sodium soy sauce
1 tbs. oyster sauce
2 tbs. dry sherry
1 tsp. sesame oil

Cut pork into 1½-x-6-inch strips. Combine hot water with brown sugar in a medium stainless steel bowl. Stir for about 2 minutes, or until brown sugar has dissolved. Add remaining ingredients, except meat, and mix thoroughly. Add pork strips and marinate for 4 hours, or overnight, in the refrigerator. Mix occasionally. Thread pork strips on 10-inch bamboo skewers and cook on a grill or under a broiler for 8 to 10 minutes. Turn and baste frequently with remaining marinade.

GARLIC MEAT LOAF

A garlic lover's delight! Serve hot or cold. Slice leftover meat loaf for fabulous sandwiches.

2 lb. ground chuck
2 cups breadcrumbs
1 egg, beaten
½ cup milk
2 medium onions, minced
2 cloves garlic, minced or squeezed
   through a press
¼ cup minced celery

¼ cup minced red or green bell
   peppers
2 tsp. Worcestershire sauce
1 tsp. dry mustard
2 tsp. minced fresh parsley
½ tsp. freshly ground pepper
¼ tsp. dried oregano
8-9 cloves garlic, thinly sliced

In a large bowl, combine all ingredients except garlic slices. Using clean hands, mix thoroughly. Pat meat mixture evenly into a meat loaf pan. Completely cover top of meat loaf with a layer of garlic slices. Bake in a preheated 350° oven for 1 hour and 15 minutes.

GARLIC-FLAVORED LAMB KABOBS

*The distinctive flavors of garlic and lamb cook together beautifully. This makes an ideal meal for an informal setting on a warm summer night. Serve with **Hummus**, page 21, **Tabouli**, page 48, and lots of small pita bread wedges.*

2 lb. lean lamb
16 oz. *Garlicky Vinaigrette*, page 52
1 tsp. dried mint, or 1 tbs. minced fresh

1 medium eggplant
2 medium red bell peppers
6 cloves garlic

Cut lamb into 1-inch cubes. Prepare *Garlicky Vinaigrette* for marinade, doubling all ingredients. Combine marinade with mint and mix well. Place cubes of lamb in a shallow bowl with marinade. Cover and refrigerate for 2 hours, or overnight. Turn occasionally in marinade. Peel eggplant and cut into 1-inch cubes. Cut peppers into 1-inch pieces. Peel and slice garlic cloves into 1/4-inch slices. Alternately thread lamb, garlic, eggplant and peppers onto bamboo skewers. Place on a medium-hot grill or under a broiler for 15 minutes. Baste with marinade and turn frequently. Serve with rice and a garden salad.

BEEF FAJITAS

This dish is fun and easy to prepare. Serve these sizzling and spicy beef strips at the table or right from the skillet. It makes a spectacular presentation for a party setting.

1 lb. flank steak
2 cloves garlic, squeezed through a
  press
½ cup olive oil
1 tbs. fresh lime juice
¼ tsp. ground cumin
1 tsp. chili powder

1 tsp. dried oregano
¼ tsp. freshly ground pepper
8 corn or flour tortillas
sliced avocado, chopped red onion,
  refried beans, diced tomatoes,
  shredded lettuce and sliced jalapeño
  peppers for filling

Cut flank steak into ¼-inch thick slices across the grain. In a small bowl, combine garlic, olive oil, lime juice, cumin, chili powder, oregano and pepper. Mix well. Add meat strips, cover and refrigerate for 6 hours, or overnight. Preheat a fajita pan or large skillet. Add marinated meat with marinade and cook on medium-high heat for 1 to 1½ minutes on each side, or until meat is cooked through. Serve with warmed tortillas and desired fillings.

ROASTED LAMB

Servings: 6

A V-shaped, heavy gauge roasting rack with adjustable sides will prevent the lamb from absorbing excess fat and works well for cooling cooked meats. Sautéed vegetables and rice make a nice accompaniment.

4 lb. leg of lamb, bone removed, tied
3 cloves garlic, squeezed through a press
¼ cup olive oil
1 tbs. minced fresh rosemary, or
   1 tsp. crushed dried
¼ tsp. dried dill weed
¼ tsp. freshly ground pepper

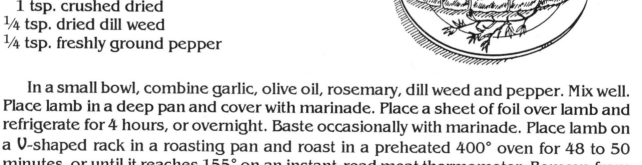

In a small bowl, combine garlic, olive oil, rosemary, dill weed and pepper. Mix well. Place lamb in a deep pan and cover with marinade. Place a sheet of foil over lamb and refrigerate for 4 hours, or overnight. Baste occasionally with marinade. Place lamb on a V-shaped rack in a roasting pan and roast in a preheated 400° oven for 48 to 50 minutes, or until it reaches 155° on an instant-read meat thermometer. Remove from oven and allow to cool for 10 minutes. Slice lamb in thin pieces to serve.

GARLIC-FLAVORED PORK CHOPS

This basic dish is easy to prepare, flavorful and very succulent.

¼ cup skim milk
¼ cup seasoned breadcrumbs
¼ tsp. garlic powder
1 tbs. freshly grated Parmesan cheese
1 tbs. chopped fresh parsley

¼ tsp. dried basil
¼ tsp. freshly ground pepper
4 pork chops, ½-inch thick
¼ cup olive oil

Pour milk into a shallow dish. In another shallow dish, combine breadcrumbs, garlic powder, Parmesan cheese, parsley, basil and pepper. Mix well. Dip chops into milk, coat with breadcrumb mixture and shake off excess. Heat olive oil in a skillet and sauté chops gently over medium heat for 5 to 6 minutes on each side, or until golden brown. Serve with mashed potatoes.

LONDON BROIL

Fresh garlic enhances the meat for a great-tasting and tender steak. Serve it with rice and salad.

1 London broil or flank steak, about 1½ lb.
2 cloves garlic, cut in half
2 tsp. vegetable or olive oil
¼ tsp. freshly ground pepper

Rub all sides of steak with garlic cloves. Coat steak with oil and sprinkle with pepper. Preheat the broiler for 10 minutes. Place steak on a lightly greased rack set 4 inches from heat. Cook steak for 6 to 7 minutes on each side. To serve, carve meat into thin slices diagonally across the grain.

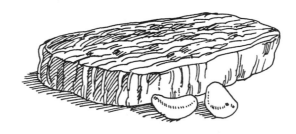

SLOPPY GARLICKY BURGERS

In 1979, the first garlic festival in Gilroy, California, attracted about 15,000 people. Recent attendance has reached over 130,000 and the crowd continues to grow each year.

¼ cup bulghur wheat
½ cup water
1 lb. ground chuck
1 medium onion, minced
4 cloves garlic, minced or squeezed
   through a press

½ cup ketchup
½ tsp. dried basil
½ tsp. freshly ground pepper
¼ tsp. chili powder
pita bread or buns

Soak bulghur wheat in water for 1 hour. Sauté meat and onions in a nonstick skillet until brown, about 5 to 6 minutes. Drain. Drain water from bulghur. Add bulghur, garlic, ketchup, basil, pepper and chili powder to meat. Mix thoroughly and cook over low heat for 5 minutes. Stir occasionally. Serve in sliced pita pockets or on buns.

LAMB CHOPS

The spicy garlic butter adds a delicious flavor to the lamb chops. It goes well with a fresh sliced tomato salad, or serve over a nutritious bed of lentils.

½ cup *Garlic Herb Butter*, page 29
4 rib or loin lamb chops, about 1¼-inch thick
4 cloves garlic, minced or squeezed through a press
½ tsp. ground dried rosemary
freshly ground pepper, optional

Prepare *Garlic Herb Butter*. Trim off excess fat on lamb chops. Place chops in a shallow dish and cover with garlic and rosemary. Refrigerate for 2 hours, or overnight. Place chops under a broiler and cook for about 4 to 5 minutes on each side. Use tongs to turn meat over — do not pierce with a fork. Continue to broil until chops are done, about 4 to 5 minutes. Remove chops from broiler. Serve garlic- and rosemary-side up. Top with *Garlic Herb Butter*, season with pepper and serve immediately on warm plates.

BROILED STEAK WITH GARLIC SAUCE

This garlic-flavored beef dish is really tender and has a wonderful flavor. It's also perfect for the backyard grill.

3 tbs. butter
2 cloves garlic, minced or squeezed
    through a press
1 tbs. olive or vegetable oil
1/2 tsp. dried oregano

1/4 tsp. ground dried rosemary
1/4 tsp. freshly ground pepper
1 (about 2 lb.) t-bone or porterhouse
    steak, 1 inch thick

Melt butter in a small saucepan. Combine melted butter with garlic, oil, oregano, rosemary and pepper. Trim excess fat from steak. Preheat the broiler for 10 minutes. Place steak on a lightly greased broiler rack set 4 inches from heat. Broil steak on each side for 5 minutes. Spread layer of garlic sauce on top of steak. Return to broiler and cook until done. To test, insert an instant-read meat thermometer into center of steak. Thermometer should read 130° for rare, 140° for medium and 160° for well done. Remove steak from broiler and serve immediately on warm serving plates.

FOREVER FAVORITE GARLICKY BEEF STEW

Servings: 8

A relaxing and easy dish to prepare that's hearty and satisfying. An ideal main course for a fall picnic or a winter buffet.

1 lb. lean beef, cut into 1-inch cubes
¼ cup flour
4 tbs. vegetable or olive oil
¾ cup celery, cut into ¾-inch pieces
1 large onion, chopped
4 cups water
1 pkg. dry onion soup mix
¼ cup red wine
12 cloves garlic, peeled
½ tsp. dried thyme
½ tsp. pepper

⅛ tsp. ground dried sage
¼ tsp. dried marjoram
¼ tsp. salt
2 medium carrots, cut into ¼-inch slices
1 red or green bell pepper, cut into
  1-inch pieces
1 cup eggplant, peeled and cut into
  1-inch cubes
4 small new potatoes, peeled and cut
  into 1-inch cubes

Coat beef with flour and set aside. Heat 2 tbs. oil in a large skillet and brown beef over medium heat for 10 to 12 minutes. Drain off fat and set aside. Heat 2 tbs. oil in a large pot or flameproof casserole. Add celery and onion and sauté for 3 minutes over medium heat. Add water and bring to a boil. Reduce heat; add soup mix, wine, garlic, spices and beef. Mix thoroughly and simmer for 1 hour and 15 minutes. Add remaining ingredients and simmer for 1 hour, or until vegetables are tender.

SIRLOIN KABOBS

*If you serve kabobs often, you can find wonderful metal skewers with decorated handles in many kitchen shops. I like to serve this succulent dish as a main course with **String Bean and Garlic Mix**, page 85, and rice.*

1/2 cup dry red wine
3 cloves garlic, minced or squeezed
  through a press
2 tbs. vegetable oil
1 tbs. grated ginger root
2 tbs. low sodium soy sauce

1/2 tsp. dried oregano
1/2 tsp. dried thyme
1/4 tsp. freshly ground pepper
1 lb. sirloin, cut into 1-x-1 1/2-inch cubes
18 mushroom caps
1 medium onion

In a large bowl, combine wine, garlic, oil, ginger, soy sauce, oregano, thyme and pepper. Mix well. Add meat and mushrooms and marinate in the refrigerator for at least 2 hours, or overnight. Cut onion into quarters and separate layers. Alternately thread meat, onion slices and mushroom caps onto presoaked bamboo skewers or metal skewers. Grill or broil 3 inches from heat for 15 minutes. Turn and baste occasionally with remaining marinade while cooking.

INDEX

Serve creative, easy, nutritious meals with nitty gritty® cookbooks

Wraps and Roll-Ups
Easy Vegetarian Cooking
Party Fare: Irresistible Nibbles
  for Every Occasion
Cappuccino/Espresso: The Book of
  Beverages
Fresh Vegetables
Cooking with Fresh Herbs
Cooking with Chile Peppers
The Dehydrator Cookbook
Recipes for the Pressure Cooker
Beer and Good Food
Unbeatable Chicken Recipes
Gourmet Gifts
From Freezer, 'Fridge and Pantry
Edible Pockets for Every Meal
Oven and Rotisserie Roasting
Risottos, Paellas and Other Rice
  Specialties
Muffins, Nut Breads and More
Healthy Snacks for Kids
100 Dynamite Desserts
Recipes for Yogurt Cheese
Sautés
Cooking in Porcelain

Casseroles
The Toaster Oven Cookbook
Skewer Cooking on the Grill
Creative Mexican Cooking
Marinades
No Salt, No Sugar, No Fat Cookbook
Quick and Easy Pasta Recipes
Cooking in Clay
Deep Fried Indulgences
The Garlic Cookbook
From Your Ice Cream Maker
The Best Pizza is Made at Home
The Best Bagels are Made at Home
Convection Oven Cookery
The Steamer Cookbook
The Pasta Machine Cookbook
The Versatile Rice Cooker
The Bread Machine Cookbook
The Bread Machine Cookbook II
The Bread Machine Cookbook III
The Bread Machine Cookbook IV:
  Whole Grains & Natural Sugars
The Bread Machine Cookbook V:
  *Favorite Recipes from 100
  Kitchens*

The Bread Machine Cookbook VI:
  *Hand-Shaped Breads from the
  Dough Cycle*
Worldwide Sourdoughs from Your
  Bread Machine
Entrées from Your Bread Machine
The New Blender Book
The Sandwich Maker Cookbook
Waffles
The Coffee Book
The Juicer Book I and II
Bread Baking
The 9 x 13 Pan Cookbook
Recipes for the Loaf Pan
Low Fat American Favorites
Healthy Cooking on the Run
Favorite Seafood Recipes
New International Fondue Cookbook
Favorite Cookie Recipes
Cooking for 1 or 2
The Well Dressed Potato
Extra-Special Crockery Pot Recipes
Slow Cooking
The Wok

**For a free catalog, write or call: Bristol Publishing Enterprises, Inc.
P.O. Box 1737, San Leandro, CA 94577 (800) 346-4889**